Richmond Football Club

1961 - 2006

Alan Skeats

Also in the same series:

Richmond Football Club 1861 - 1925

Richmond Football Club 1925 - 1961

First published in Great Britain in 2007 by Richmond Football Club,
Kew Foot Road, Richmond, TW9 2SS.

A catalogue record for this title is available from the British Library.

ISBN 978-0-9554842-0-9

Typesetting and Design by TMA Ltd.

Proofreader (all enquiries) Michael Hodgson-Hess.

Printed and bound in Poland by Trade Print Europe Ltd.

Prologue

It was in a rare moment of historical uncertainty in 1999 that we formed the Richmond FC Archives and History House (RASH). Andy Quigley, Ted Brown, Alan Skeats and myself are it and remain so. Our search for a researcher and author to write our last forty plus years fell, after a couple of refusniks, to the indomitable and effervescent Alan Skeats. His work, research and attention to detail have been outstanding - just like his service to the club he so loves.

The style follows the first two noble editions in accounting for our 1st XV on the park and, occasionally, our administrators off it. It is a book of reference, a 'joie de vivre' of the Richmond Football Club and, above all, it is where our blood runs old gold, red and black.

Richmond's story is stunning, unique, and a triumph over disaster of Herculean proportions. No wonder we are a friendly place where the game of rugby flourishes.

Thank you Alan, may Richmond Floreat Ubique,

Tony Hallett
President, Richmond F.C.
30th November 2006

Acknowledgements

I am most grateful to the following people from within the club who have dug deep into their memories (and their attics) to provide information not easily acquired through other sources:

Roddy Adams, John Aylwin, Vic Balchin, Richard Boggon, Ian Botes, Ted Brown, David Buchanan, David Chisnall, Simon Codrington, Vinny Codrington, Tony Dorman, Sue Dorrington, Tony Hallett, Mark Holman, Harry Hooper, Pat Lavery, Peter Moore, Michael Oliviera, Andy Quigley, Robin Robins, Tony Stansfield, Mike Stobart, Robert Vallings, Tony Vyvyan, Phil Williams and Nigel Wilson, with special thanks to Jim Holloway for his searching amongst local micro-files at the library and to Lucy Jones who had the unenviable job of typing from my longhand.

Help has also been given freely by others outside the club and their assistance is very much appreciated:

Mack Brown and Jack Dun (Melrose RFC), Paul Dobson (South Africa), Chris Edwards (Empangeni), Ross Hamilton and Staff (R.F.U.), Bryan Lynch (former Member), Graeme Mahler and John Simmins (R.A.A.), Jim Oldroyd and John Vale (Surrey C.R.F.U.), Laing Speirs (Gala R.F.C.), Robert Spaight (former player), David Spyer (London Society of Referees and Middlesex C.R.F.U.)

Most importantly, this book could never have happened without the support of Doreen who has suffered months of a lounge littered with writes, re-writes and the offerings given by those mentioned above - not to mention the frequent tearing of hair which she has had to suffer. To all who have made it possible therefore, I give my unqualified thanks.

Alan Skeats

Photographic Acknowledgements: We thank the many contributors who have given their permission for photographs to be used in programmes, newsletters and other club publications. Special thanks to Colin McMichael, also Keith Wigmore, John Cornish, Dave Jackson, Tim Mott, CPCL, rugbymatters.net, ITV and many club members.

Contents

Foreword

The previous two histories of Richmond Football Club covering the period 1861 to 1961 (the Centenary Year) were written strictly chronologically. However, much has evolved in the game of Rugby Union Football over the past forty years (from the advent of the Gate Taking Clubs' Association through to the Senior Clubs' Association and the inception of the leagues and professionalism) that, although year by year results, "incidents" and memorable matches are dealt with in that way, my objective is to classify changes under separate chapters.

Changes in how Richmond is run started back in 1951 when John Megaw (later knighted), former Irish International and a High Court Judge, planned to depart from his predecessor's tradition by not dying in office. He asserted that too many good members of the club had been precluded from high office by a long life presidency term and proposed instead that, elected and re-elected annually, a President should serve for a maximum of three years only. This policy has been maintained since then, except by your compiler who "suffered" for five years - goodness knows why!

In 1961 another major change took place when our Captain, Bill Munks, argued successfully that, although virtually all our players came from leading public schools, the club should be open to all "good chaps", whatever their background. However, a few years later I recall a President trying to reject local grammar school players, even though in some instances they were better players than some of their public school counterparts. Additionally, until the late 1970s, potential non-playing members of the club had to be vetted personally by the incumbent Secretary.

Although this book emphasises the senior area of Richmond over the past forty years, the club has always been justly proud of its many junior players as well as the numerous hard working unpaid officials who have given their all for us.

Finally, the Acknowledgements page lists those to whom I am indebted for their assistance and research in compiling this book. I hope that those following down the years will keep club records in good order so that future historians will have all at their fingertips.

Alan Skeats
2006

"God and good angels fight on Richmond's side." (Shakespeare)

Chapter One

The Sixties

1961/2

Richmond's centenary year saw Charles R. Hopwood, (England trialist, Barbarians and Middlesex which he captained) re-elected as President to serve with Frank Bisgood T.D in his twelfth year as Secretary, John Black as Treasurer (since 1954/5) and Bill Munks as Captain for the second time.

On the pitch, the year started in auspicious fashion at Twickenham when Richmond played an International XV selected by the President of the R.F.U., Major-General R.G.S. Hobbs, Lieutenant Governor of Chelsea Royal Hospital and a Richmond member. The array of stars to play against us was formidable. The side consisted of Ken Scotland (London Scottish and Scotland); Tony O'Reilly (Dolphin and Ireland), James Shackleton (London Scottish and Scotland), Iain Laughland (London Scottish and Scotland), Arthur Smith (Edinburgh Wanderers and Scotland), Philip Horrocks-Taylor (Leicester and England), John Williams (Old Millhillians and England), Gordon Bendon (Wasps and England), John Wackett (Rosslyn Park and England), Norman Bruce (London Scottish and Scotland), David Marques (Harlequins and England), Gareth Payne (London Welsh and Wales), Richard Boggan (St Thomas' Hospital, Richmond and Middlesex), Derek Morgan (Medicals and England) and John Leleu (Swansea and Wales). Against this might Richmond fielded Roger Segal; Peter Thorning, Ted Wates, Mike Weston, Richard Mayle; Geoffrey Windsor-Lewis, Steve Smith, Bill Munks, Pat Orr, Mike Reuben, Paul Charteris, Graham (Fruity) Fox, Brian Stoneman, Peter Ryan and Bobby Burns. Mike Weston and Steve Smith had gained caps for England and Geoffrey Windsor-Lewis for Wales, whilst Brian Stoneman remained arguably one of the best players never to be capped by England.

Only late scores by Arthur Smith secured victory for the President's XV by a margin of 28-19. The Press recorded that it was one of the best games of rugby football ever seen on the ground.

Three days later Richmond beat Old Cranleighans 35-8 at home then went away a week later to win 18-6 over Croydon and District before losing at home 3-12 to Northampton. Other September results were; Bedford at home (won 34-11) and Rosslyn Park away (lost 9-12). October too proved a month of mixed fortunes, the outcomes being a loss away to London Welsh (6-14), a win at home over Leicester (24-3), a loss against Oxford University (3-16) at

Iffley Road and an away win (13-0) over London University.

The last win came two days after the Centenary Dinner at the Café Royal, when speakers included the Rt. Hon. Lord Evershed M.R. (Master of the Rolls), Lord of Appeal in Ordinary, who played for the Extra A in the 1920s, the Hon. Sir John Megaw C.B.E (High Court Judge), Richmond's former Irish International, and His Honour Judge Aarvold. In view of the fact that the law was so strongly represented, the annual Richmond Record observed that "the roll throwing fraternity nobly refrained from any activity."

November was also an in-and-out month during which we lost away to Llanelli (5-17) and at home to Harlequins (0-9) but then, in two home games, beat London Scottish (14-3) and scored 12 points to Swansea's 11. The last month of the year saw the start of an unbeaten run which went through to the beginning of March with a draw at home (6-6) against London Irish, then three wins away - over St Mary's Hospital (26-3), Blackheath (18-6) and Harlequins (20-0).

Still away for two games at the start of January, the club chalked up successes against Guy's Hospital (24-3) and U.S Portsmouth (19-0) followed by a home win over Cambridge University (9-0) and an away one at Rugby where the score was 43-3 in our favour. February provided a one hundred percent record during a month of all home games when defeats were inflicted on Wasps (21-3), Blackheath (6-5), Bristol (16-9) and O.M.Ts (16-8). March started well with a 16-8 victory over London Scottish but then two away fixtures were lost against Gloucester (11-14) and Moseley (8-21) before, under floodlights away, we beat Northampton (3-0) and then won 11-0 at home against U.S Portsmouth and 38-0 away versus Old Elthamians. The last match of the season, away at New Brighton, saw Richmond lose 0-6. At Easter the 1st XV (missing 6 regular first team players) lost in a match described as "the best seen in Cork for some years" by 19-22 to Cork Constitution whilst the A XV notched up two victories - over the Danish National XV (36-12) and Roskilde (21-3). The players featured on the team photograph that year beside Bill Munks were John Aves, Bobby Burns, Robin Butler (later Secretary to the Cabinet and Head of the Home Civil Service and currently Lord Butler of Brockwell G.C.B, C.V.O, Master of University College, Oxford), Paul Charteris, Brian Dykes, Tony Fitch, Graham Fox, David Froud, Tony Hole, Tony Holmes, Richard Moyle, Pat Orr, Ian Palmer-Lewis, Charles Pearce, Mike Pope, Roger Segal, Steve Smith, Brian Stoneman, Peter Thorning, Ted Wates, Mike Weston and Geoffrey Windsor-Lewis, the last two being currently Treasurer and Secretary of the Barbarians respectively.

The following players achieved representative honours during the season - Mike Weston (British Lions, England, Barbarians and captaincy of Durham),

Bill Munks (Barbarians), Peter Thorning (Barbarians and Devon), Steve Smith (Barbarians and captaincy of Hampshire), Tony Hole (Barbarians, Surrey), Brian Stoneman and Pat Orr (London Counties and Middlesex), Ted Wates and Bobby Burns (Surrey), Richard Moyle (Army and Cornwall), Richard Boyson and Graham Fox (Middlesex), David Murphy (RAF), Mike Pope (Berkshire), Tony Fitch (Hertfordshire) and Geoffrey Windsor-Lewis (Oxfordshire).

1962/3

Charles Hopwood was again re-elected as President, but the invaluable secretaryship of Frank Bisgood came to an end and Fred Lovell, former player and 1st Team Secretary, took over that onerous task. The redoubtable John Black continued as Treasurer to keep an eye on the purse strings. The Captaincy passed to Ted Wates. He regrettably had to resign from that position during the season and Geoffrey Windsor-Lewis stepped nobly into the breach.

The other leading players that season were Tony Boyd-Smith, Bobby Burns, Robin Butler, John Collingwood, Peter Cook, Tony Fitch, Graham Fox, Stan Good, Tony Hole, David Kilmister, Pat Orr, Bob Poole, Mike Pope, Steve Smith, Brian Stoneman, Peter Thorning and Tony Vyvyan.

The season opened with an away match v Old Cranleighans where we won 35-3 but the next two away games showed losses against Northampton (3-9) and Bedford (8-19). The losing sequence continued when, at The Athletic Ground, Rosslyn Park won 24-12 and London Welsh outscored us 19-0. At Leicester, the home side beat us 21-3 before we finally won at home when visiting Oxford University lost 9-15. Facing Cambridge University at home, we capitulated again, going down 3-17 but, also at home, Llanelli were seen off, 18-0. Harlequins triumphed at Twickenham 21-3 but then came a run of five wins, at home to London Scottish (6-5), away to Swansea (8-6) and London Irish (9-3), after which Richmond beat St Mary's Hospital 24-3 and Blackheath 12-3.

From that last game on 12th January, there is no record of any games played until 2nd March, the weather presumably being very bad. The first game in March was against London Scottish away and we bettered our previous score against them with a 14-6 result.

A trip to The Reddings gave us a 16-0 win over Moseley, but travelling Gosforth came down and returned with the spoils, 18-8. Bath away was our last loss (12-17) before a cancellation against Coventry brought three wins, over Saracens in north London 17-0, New Brighton at home 16-3 and, also at home, Harlequins 5-0.

The Vikings tripped away to West Germany resulting in a 3-3 draw with

Hanover Ricklingen (1908), a loss against an infantry divisional XV (all tourists apparently too tight to record the score) and, finally, another draw - this time 6-6 versus R.A.O.C. XV at Bielefeld.

Representative honours that season were gained by Mike Weston (England Captain in New Zealand, and Durham), Steve Smith (London Counties, Hampshire-Captain), Peter Thorning (England Trials, Devon), Pat Orr (London Counties, Middlesex), Geoffrey Windsor-Lewis (Captain of Oxfordshire), Brian Stoneman (Middlesex, Oxford University), Paul Charteris (London Clubs, Surrey), F. (Sam) Morris (London Counties, Hampshire), Frank Burns (England Trials, Cumberland and Westmorland), John Collingwood (Oxford University) and, for Hampshire, David (Dai) Hawkes and Eric Lipscombe and for Surrey, Mike Pope, Bobby Burns and Tony Hole.

During the season, we lost Richard Boggon who went off to doctor in St Helena. He had not heard that Napoleon was dead!

1963/4

The Presidency was assumed by Frank Mennim who schooled at St Bees in Lancashire and was our courageous full back in the 1930s. He was supported by a new Secretary in Neville Pinnington, one of our consistent backs in the 1950s, and the 'traditional' Treasurer John Black. The captaincy resided in the firm hands of Steve Smith who, as scrum-half, was capped by England during the season, along with representative honours with South Eastern Counties and Hampshire. South Africa capped Tommy Bedford.

Other representative honours were gained by Colin Allan (Cornwall), Frank Burns (Cumberland and Westmoreland and the RAF), Robin Butler (Captaincy of the Civil Service), Paul Charteris (Surrey), John Collingwood (Eastern Counties), Peter Cook (Barbarians, South Eastern Counties, Surrey), Peter Eastwood (Barbarians, Combined Services, South Eastern Counties, Hampshire, Army), Dai Hawkes (Hampshire), Tony Hole (Surrey), Alan Hunt (Kent), Tom Jones (Combined Services and the Navy), Richard Moyle (Cornwall), Pat Orr (Barbarians, Middlesex), Roger Palin (Combined Services, RAF), John Stevenson (Sussex), Brian Stoneman (Middlesex), Peter Thorning (S.W. Counties and Devon), David Webster (Lancashire) and Geoffrey Windsor-Lewis (Southern Counties and Oxfordshire).

The team photograph featured the Captain and Colin Allan, Bobby Burns, Robin Butler, Bill Campbell, Paul Charteris, John Collingwood, Peter Cook, Ken Ebenezer, Mike Elphick, Dai Hawkes, Tony Hole, Pat Orr, Ernie Preece, Brian Stoneman, Peter Thorning, Ted Wates and David Webster.

The season started well with three wins at home - against Saracens

(15-3), Cork Constitution (39-20) and Northampton (13-11) but then visitors Bedford went home 20-3 winners as did Leicester 11-8. These fixtures were followed by two matches against universities, both away; Oxford lost to us 9-22, as did London, 3-47. At Stradey, Llanelli were outscored 13-5 before a home crash to Harlequins 8-13. London Scottish were entertained and we beat our guests 24-6 but Swansea went back to Wales with a 16-0 scoreline under their belt.

The in-and-out season continued with Rosslyn Park at home registering 14 points to our 3, London Irish coming to us to lose 0-8 before we went down 0-6 at St Mary's Hospital. At Twickenham, Harlequins failed to score against our 8 points and there was no score against us the following week either, when we beat Guys Hospital 15-0. A visit to Portsmouth saw United Services run out victors 13-6 whilst, away at Waterloo, the Lancastrians gave us best, 11-22.

At the beginning of February, Wasps visited Richmond and lost by the narrow margin of 0-5 and, a week later, Blackheath went home with a 6-3 win. Another three home fixtures followed, all recording victories - over Bristol 14-6, O.M.Ts 60-3 and Coventry 10-6. Even travel to London Scottish was successful as we won 16-13 but, at New Brighton, the home XV stole the match 10-9.

To finish the season, two games at home showed a win over Moseley 5-0 but a final loss was to Neath 6-15.

At the season's end in Spain, on a trip to support the British Industries Fair, the 1st XV thrashed San Buoyano to the tune of 66-9 and Barcelona University Club, 58-8.

1964/5

The team at the top of the club - President, Secretary, Treasurer and Captain remained the same as the season before and an Executive Committee was formed, chaired by Frank Mennim. It was a splendid year in which the 1st XV registered twenty-four wins with only nine losses; scoring 522 points with 262 against.

Three of the club players were capped by England during the season - Peter Cooke (who also got a Barbarians cap and represented Surrey), Mike Weston, plus another Barbarians cap and captaincy of Durham and Steve Richards (who, in addition, appeared for London Counties and Middlesex). Five other members of the side captained their counties - Roger Godfrey (London Counties - he also played for Kent), John Collingwood (Eastern Counties), Ian Palmer-Lewis (Staffordshire) and Geoffrey Windsor-Lewis (Oxfordshire), while Stan Good and Colin McFadyean led St

Luke's College and Loughborough Colleges respectively.

Other representative honours were gained by Brian Stoneman (England Trials, Rest of England v Champion County, Barbarians, London Counties, Middlesex), Ken Ebenezer (Surrey), Pat Orr (Barbarians, Middlesex), Jonathan Harvey (Cambridge University), Dick Bateman and Ernie Preece (Middlesex), Peter Eastwood (Hampshire, Combined Services, Army), Bobby Burns and Dai Hawkes (Hampshire), Bill Campbell and Alan Hunt (Kent), Paul Charteris (Surrey), Tony Kitchin (Hertfordshire), Jim Glover (Cornwall), Simon Jones (Sussex), Brian Siggins (Connaught), Peter Thorning (Devon), Howard Waller (Eastern Counties), David Webster (Lancashire), Tom Jones (Combined Services, Navy), Roger Palin (Combined Services, RAF), Mike Stear (RAF) and Mike Wilkes (Army).

On 9th September we kicked off with a 12-11 win over Saracens away before overwhelming Old Alleynians at home by 55-0. Oxford were beaten 19-16, also at home.

Two away matches meant an 8-17 loss at Northampton but, again in the East Midlands, a 23-5 win at Goldington Road, Bedford was followed by a home win over London Welsh 22-14. Back in the East Midlands there was a good 27-3 win against Leicester and then four home games produced three wins and a loss, results being Oxford University 18-3, Cambridge University 6-11, Rosslyn Park 16-3 and Llanelli 14-9. Harlequins were faced away and we lost 0-3, and then the home match versus London Scottish gave them the edge 14-3.

Now two games away from home produced an 8-19 loss to Swansea then a 15-6 win over London Irish. A string of five matches at The Athletic Ground gave four wins and a loss, the games ending v. St Mary's Hospital 12-8, v. Blackheath 3-11, v. Harlequins 8-6, v. Guys Hospital 15-8 and v. US Portsmouth 9-3.

An away game against Old Merchant Taylors gave us a 27-3 win and we followed that with a home victory over Waterloo, 26-15. The last Saturday in January for whatever reason was blank, but February started with Wasps 23 Richmond 3 at Sudbury. Another two away games gave us no joy as Blackheath won 10-6 and Bristol won 11-5.

Harrogate were visitors but suffered a 3-37 loss before London Scottish, in their home fixture, won 14-0. Away in Birmingham, Richmond then produced a 17-9 win over Moseley. The last five games gave a good end-of-season run for us as we beat Gosforth 8-3 at home, Bath (26-12) and Neath (8-6) both away, with a final fling in Ireland when two more victories followed - versus Cork Constitution (20-3) and University College, Cork (26-8).

The Vikings were in Germany yet again - this time further afield in Berlin but stopping en route to play Hanover Ricklingen (1908) again, winning 16-11. Then on to the final destination when RAF Gatow were thrashed 65-3 but, as is normal with these tours, no record was made of the winning score versus Combined Services.

Leading appearances were made by Colin Allan, Ian Brown, Bobby Burns, Robin Butler, Paul Charteris, John Collingwood, Peter Cook, Peter Eastwood, Ken Ebenezer, Simon Jones, Tom Jones, Mike Lee, Ernie Preece, Chris Ralston, Steve Richards, Robin Robins, Steve Smith, Brian Stoneman, Peter Thorning, Howard Waller, Ted Wates and David Webster.

1965/6

The President Frank Mennim was now supported by John Powell-Rees, a Swansea man and former Vikings Captain, as secretary and Treasurer John Black. The Chairmanship of the Executive still lay with the President. Paul Charteris assumed the captaincy but, unfortunately, a serious injury the season before limited him to only intermittent appearances before Christmas. Hamstring and knee problems forced him to resign and Tony Hole became skipper for the rest of the season. Robin Butler, a stalwart of previous years, also had a knee problem and did not appear at all, nor did Bobby Burns (injury and work commitments in Portsmouth). Steve Smith, now working in the Midlands, was turning out for Moseley. A number of other players had badly interrupted seasons but, in spite of all the setbacks, the club lost only three times before the New Year.

The most used players were Colin Allan, John Aylwin, Dick Bateman, Alan Blake, Ian Brown, Bobby Bruce, Paul Charteris, John Collingwood, Peter Cook, Tony Davies, Peter Eastwood, Ken Ebenezer, Tony Hole, Ian Moffat, Ian Palmer-Lewis, Ernie Preece, Chris Ralston, Peter (Winkle) Raymond, Steve Richards, Robin Robins, Brian Stoneman, Alistair Thom and Howard Waller.

The opening game resulted in a 26-3 win over Oxford away followed by a good victory, 13-3, against Racing Club de France after which our guests opted much more enthusiastically for whisky than for our excellent local beer. A third win on the trot came when we beat Saracens 11-8 at home but then came the first loss, to Northampton, 8-9, on our ground. Still at home, we won 30-6 against Bedford.

October was a good month as Leicester came to us and lost 3-13, then again we supported a British Industries Fair, this time in Italy, where we beat Milan and District XV 21-6. Two matches against universities followed when, at Iffley Road, we beat Oxford 19-13 and, at Motspur Park, we came out on top against London (20-8).Then away in Roehampton, Rosslyn Park gave us best, 5-11.

Away to Llanelli we won 8-3 after which Harlequins were seen off 13-3 at home. But then, in a home game with London Scottish, we crashed 0-21. Swansea were our visitors and lost 3-9 and, also at home, London Irish crashed to us 5-27. Four away games were good for Richmond as we beat St Mary's Hospital 17-12, drew with Blackheath 9-9, won at Guys Hospital 11-0 and had a 28-3 victory v US Portsmouth.

Coventry were our next visitors and shared the spoils 16-16 but an away game with Wasps resulted in a 3-9 loss before a tight game at home when Blackheath lost 0-3. Bristol travelled and took the spoils 16-8. O.M.Ts visited and lost 3-17 but, away at London Scottish, we lost 13-21 and then, facing the "auld enemy" again at Hawick, we went down 6-38.

Moseley won a cliff-hanger 14-13 at The Athletic Ground and, again at home, Richmond saw off Bath 32-11 as we did the following week when Neath departed 3-8 down. A trip to New Brighton brought a 3-6 loss and, finally, fellow Lancastrians Sale had an 11-9 win down here. The Vikings toured the Loire, beating St Leger 23-8 and Cosne 13-8.

Pride of place in representative honours went to Mike Weston (British Lions, England, Durham) and Brian Stoneman (Barbarians, London Counties, Middlesex). These two were followed by a host of others namely Ken Ebenezer (London Counties and Surrey), Chris Ralston and Steve Richards (London Counties and Middlesex), Colin Allan, John Aylwin, Dick Bateman, Paul Charteris and Ernie Preece (all Middlesex), Ian Moffat (Rest of England v Champion County and Oxfordshire), Bobby Bruce and Tony Davies (both Berkshire), Bill Hadman (Oxford University), Roger Palin (Northumberland, Combined Services and also Captain of the RAF), Peter Eastwood (Hampshire, Army), Bobby Burns (Hampshire), Bill Campbell (Kent), John Collingwood (Captain, Eastern Counties for whom Howard Waller also featured), Chris Jennins (Lancashire), Jonathan Harvey (Somerset), Simon Jones (Sussex), Ian Palmer-Lewis (Hertfordshire), Geoffrey Windsor-Lewis as Captain of Oxfordshire and Tony Smith (Cumberland and Westmoreland).

1966/7

Long time member Tom Rider became President; Andrew Page, a full back of a few years ago, was the new Secretary; John Black continued as Treasurer, Executive Committee Chairmanship passed to John Riley, who played for Waterloo and Lancashire before performing for Richmond, and the role of Captain was taken on by Brian Stoneman who distinguished himself with a masterly display of oratory at the annual club dinner. This was a year when Oxford University provided us with a whole host of talent, including Nigel

Wilson together with Jon Gabitass in the New Year, and the Varsity's whole back row of Tony Bucknall, Tommy Bedford (later a famed Springbok) and Bill Hadman.

There were five wins to start the season - over Saracens 21-3 (away), Racing Club de France 39-14 (even after a dousing of Pernod in Paris), Cambridge 14-5 (home), Northampton 11-0 (away), before a home match against East Africa saw a massive 65-0 triumph.

Bedford stopped the success with a 17-8 victory over us at Goldington Road, we managed a 9-9 draw with London Welsh at home, suffered two more losses 3-22 (away) and 0-5 (home) against Leicester and Oxford University respectively. Against Cambridge University at The Athletic Ground, we won 11-8 followed by a 9-8 win over Rosslyn Park, also at home. Then we had two draws, 6-6 with Llanelli (note the new spelling) at home and away against Harlequins 3-3. Not a good time, as then London Scottish put 23 points on us against our nothing in a home game before we went down 3-6 to Nottingham in Beeston.

The balance was slightly restored by three wins - v London Irish 32-0 (away), St Mary's Hospital 28-0 (home) and Blackheath 12-0 (home). An in-and-out season continued when Harlequins beat us 6-0 at Richmond and Coventry scored 9 points to our 6 at Coundon Road. Against albeit lesser opposition, Richmond outpointed US Portsmouth 15-9 (home), Army 21-0 (home) and Old Merchant Taylors 16-6 (away) before succumbing in a home match to Waterloo, 0-3. In the US Portsmouth team were two sub-lieutenants, Royal Navy, Leigh Merrick and Tony Hallett. Both were to join Richmond, Leigh to become a 1st XV member and Hallett a distinguished Heavy. Their contributions to Club and Country subsequently are recorded later. One victory at Sudbury over Wasps 11-9 did not mean that we got back on winning course as we then lost at the Rectory Field, 0-5 to Blackheath, and 8-17 to Bristol (away). In the matches that followed, victories were gained over Camborne 51-6 (home), London Scottish 14-10 (away), Moseley 8-6 (away) and Gosforth 9-0 (home) before Richmond suffered a heavy 0-25 defeat against Neath at The Gnoll.

The Southern Hemisphere kept us down to a 21-17 win at The Athletic Ground before on tour we beat Bridgwater and Albion 24-3 after which the season was rounded off in France (again!) with a brace of wins over Maurs 16-8 and Perigueux 27-14 - both at Terasson where, because of the number of university graduates in our XV, the local paper described us as " Les Universitaires de Richmond". The Vikings travelled to Eire and beat Cork Constitution 2nd XV 24-6, Skibereen 13-6 and Bandon 24-17 after which, when approaching London Airport, the flight captain was heard to announce

"Well played Powell-Rees and Richmond F.C. We look forward to having you on KLM again."

The year's leading players under Brian Stoneman were Colin Allan, John Aylwin, Dicky Bateman, Tommy Bedford, Terry Brooke, Jim Brownlee, Tony Bucknall, John Collingwood, Peter Cook, Gavin Cormack, Bill Hadman, Jonathan Harvey, Robin Jolliffe, Tom Jones, Benny Lee, Roger Lewis, Ian Moffatt, Ernie Preece, Chris Ralston, Steve Richards, Howard Waller and Robin Whitcomb.

Steve Richards played for England, London Counties, South Eastern Counties and Middlesex were Brian Stoneman (also Middlesex) and Tommy Bedford were Barbarians. Tommy Bedford was also Captain of Oxford University over four other Richmond members Bill Hadman, Steve James, Tony Bucknall and Jon Gabitass, who also played for South Western Counties. Chris Ralston played for London Counties and Middlesex for whom John Aylwin also appeared. Peter Eastwood played in the Army XV and Hampshire where he was joined by Bobby Burns. Surrey Caps were awarded to Terry Brooke, Peter Cook and Ken Ebenezer, Sussex caps to Simon Jones and Nigel Parker and Eastern Counties caps to John Collingwood and Howard Waller. The following players also represented their counties - Ian Moffatt (Oxfordshire), Bobby Bruce and Tony Davies (Berkshire), Jim Brownlee (Durham), Ian Palmer-Lewis (Hertfordshire). Recognition too for Steve Petzing (Army) and Keith Parry (RAF).

In September 1966, the Daily Express suggested that Richmond's front row of Brian Stoneman (The Whale), John Aylwin (The Judge) and Tom Jones (The Cat) should be England's front row.

Regrettably, the season saw the deaths of three members; Charles Hopwood who, apart from his achievements on and off the pitch in earlier years, had overseen the building of the new stand after the fire of 1956; of Ken Ebenezer who met an untimely end in a motor accident; and R.E Godfrey who had captained the club in 1906/7.

1967/8

The offices of President and Secretary both remained in the safe hands of Tom Rider and Andrew Page respectively, with the everlasting John Black still steadying the money. John Riley retained the reins on the Executive, whilst the effervescent New Zealander, Gavin Cormack, took over the responsibility of Captain. The leading players were Colin Allan, Chris Ball, Dicky Bateman, Alan Blake, Tommy Bedford, Terry Brooke, John Collingwood, Peter Cook, Freddie Craig, Mike Davis, Stuart Fleming, Bill Hadman, Jonathan Harvey,

Dai Hawkes, Robin Jolliffe, Bennie Lee, Ernie Preece, Chris Ralston, Steve Richards, Brian Stoneman, Howard Waller, Robin Whitcomb and Dean Wotherspoon. Richmond had now nominated a club coach so these players came under the direction of Johnny Watterson, sports master of Hampton School.

The season started with four home matches and the results were versus Streatham-Croydon, a win by 34-0; Racing Club de France 18-3 to us; Northampton 8-13 and Bedford 29-3. At Roehampton we won 11-9 v Rosslyn Park but at Old Deer Park crashed 3-28 to London Welsh.

Leicester were met at home and Richmond won 13-0 before Oxford University at Iffley Road outscored us 12-6 followed by a north-eastern trip to share the spoils 3-3 with Gosforth. The game at Llanelli was cancelled because of an International before we engaged in four games at home - showing a 75% result as Harlequins 16-12, London Scottish 19-9 and Swansea 16-10 were overcome but London Irish had a 21-11 result in their favour.

Bad weather spoiled the match with St Mary's Hospital at Teddington but we won 16-9 at Blackheath then again a blank Saturday as the away game with Harlequins was called off due to the climate. On Boxing Day, we entertained a Blackheath President's XV but went down 8-9. Another loss followed when Coventry returned to the Midlands as 17-16 victors.

Away to the south coast where our hosts U.S Portsmouth (Hallett and Merrick again!) gave us best 8-21 but another weather break meant the cancellation of the fixture with the Army at Aldershot, then in Cambridge we beat the university 12-6. Travel again, this time to Liverpool where, by the odd point, we lost 16-17 to Waterloo.

The Athletic Ground was the scene for the next four Saturdays and again a 75% record - with wins over Wasps 18-3 and Blackheath 11-8. Bristol were then the victors 11-9 but we recovered to beat O.M.Ts 29-6. Travelling to London Scottish gave Richmond the edge 6-3 and, at Imber Court, Metropolitan Police succumbed 12-18 a week before we lost at home 11-24 to Moseley.

The season finished with another three home fixtures starting with a 3-8 loss to Bath followed by a win over Saracens 21-3 but ending with a 10-11 defeat by Neath.

The players who distinguished themselves and the club by gaining representative honours were:- at International level, Terry Brooke (England, also chosen for the Barbarians and Surrey) and Tommy Bedford (South Africa, also gaining recognition with the Barbarians and Oxford University). England Trials showed the appearance of Steve Richards, who was also on the England tour of Canada and was selected for Middlesex, and Brian

Stoneman, who also played for Middlesex. Another Middlesex selection, Chris Ralston, was an England Trials reserve. Blues at Oxford University were awarded to John Croker and Nigel Wilson whilst county appearances were made by Jim Brownlee (Durham), Peter Cook (Surrey), John Collingwood (Eastern Counties), Stuart Fleming (Cheshire), Jonathan Harvey (Dorset & Wilts), Dai Hawkes (Hampshire), Robin Jolliffe (Middlesex) and Howard Waller (Eastern Counties).

One special match during the season was against Wellington College. This was played in November on their ground to commemorate the first fixture in 1868 which Richmond had won by 1 goal to nil. This year's match result is not recorded.

1968/9

Gavin Cormack, having been given a successful "send off" dinner, retired to his native Antipodes but Tom Rider and Andrew Page stayed on as President and Secretary respectively. The Chairmanship of the Executive was still held by John Riley and John Black continued as Treasurer. The captaincy was taken over by Ernie Preece with coach John Watterson at his side. They saw their XV suffer fifteen losses offset by eleven wins and one draw.

There were four away matches to kick off the season resulting in a loss to Saracens 3-8, a win over Racing Club de France 21-19, a loss to Northampton 15-2 and a victory at Bedford 13-3. The first home match against London Welsh saw Richmond go down 13-17 and, away at Welford Road, Leicester won 28-19. Two home matches, against Oxford University (won 11-8) and Cambridge University (lost 8-16), presaged the club's ability to be up one minute and down the next. Next, two losses - at home to Llanelli 3-14 and away at Harlequins 16-25, preceded a win over co-tenants London Scottish (a home fixture) 6-3 but, at St Helens a week later, Swansea managed a 16-11 victory. At The Athletic Ground, Rosslyn Park were beaten 10-0 followed by a win at Sunbury over London Irish 27-6 then, in the last fixture in 1968 (two December matches were called off), Richmond succumbed at home to Blackheath, 8-17.

The New Year started with a trio of victories - against US Portsmouth 16-14, the Army 18-3, both at home and, at O.M.Ts, 29-0. Then the rot set in and Waterloo beat us 10-3 at home after which we lost 8-3 at Sudbury against Wasps before the next three games - against Blackheath, Bristol and Headingley, were called off due to wintry conditions. When play resumed again in March, London Scottish at home beat us 3-0, Moseley at The Reddings beat us 27-11 and, at home, Gosforth were victors over us 6-3.

An away draw 6-6 with Bath and a loss at Coundon Road, Coventry by a scoreline of 8-14 were in front of two late season wins, both away - at Streatham-Croydon 14-8 and Neath 21-13.

Pre-eminent players during the season were Colin Allan, John Aylwin, Peter Baron, Dicky Bateman, Alan Blake, Ian Botes, Tony Bucknall, John Croker, Stuart Fleming, Jonathan Harvey, Dai Hawkes, Peter Hearn, Nigel Hook, Tony Kitchin, Pat Lavery, Bennie Lee, Ernie Preece, Chris Ralston, Colin Simpson, Chris Waterman and Nigel Wilson.

Representative honours were won by Tony Bucknall (England Trials, Eastern Counties), Chris Ralston (London Counties, Middlesex), Rod Mulvey (Oxford University), Robin Jolliffe, John Croker and Steve Richards (Middlesex). Also Dorset and Wilts (Jonathan Harvey), Eastern Counties (Howard Waller) Hampshire (Ian Botes), Hertfordshire (Tony Kitchin), Surrey (David Atkinson and Robin Whitcomb) and, for Sussex, Andrew Peters. In the midst of his missionary work in Asia, our 1963/4 captain, Steve Smith, was capped by India. Off the field, the club members were recognised by the elevation of Sir John Megaw to Lord Justice of Appeal and the knighthood of Oliver Chesterton, who is still a member.

The year was rounded off by a highly successful tour to the USA, details of which can be found in the chapter on Major Tours.

1969/70

The Presidency passed to Frank Bisgood, Secretary for so many years and touch-judge ("another few yards Frank!") of distinction, and the Secretaryship to Alan Skeats, a former Vikings Secretary and full back who played for the Army (Egypt), Notts and Northampton prior to joining Richmond. Treasurer John Black still continued in his post, as did John Riley in Executive Chairman capacity, with the Anglo-Scot (of Brazilian background) Colin Allan installed as Captain, again helped by Johnny Watterson as Coach.

This was to be another season of mixed fortunes. There were a few wins occasionally strung together but they were punctuated by losses in many games which Richmond should have won. An opening defeat at home against Saracens by 8-13 preceded a win away at Southend by 28 points to 15 and a home victory over Northampton 6-3 before we fell away at The Athletic Ground when Bedford won convincingly 27-14. At Old Deer Park, London Welsh scored 25 points to our 3 but we recovered at home versus Leicester to win 22-19. Three away matches ensued with a win over Oxford University 11-8 but two defeats, at Gosforth 8-14 and Llanelli 3-32.

More trouble at home when Richmond lost to Harlequins 12-18 and

London Scottish 3-16 but, at the end of November, victories were recorded by 17-6 over Swansea and 17-3 against Rosslyn Park but London Irish came to us and outscored us 11-3. Then we beat St Mary's Hospital away 17-8.

Throughout December and January we were not at home and recorded three successive defeats at the hands of Blackheath 6-22, Harlequins 14-28 and U.S Portsmouth 5-6 before there were three victories in a row over the Army 6-3, Cambridge University 23-9 and Waterloo 14-3. At The Athletic Ground, Coventry narrowly won 13-12 and, also at home, we beat Wasps 6-3. A week's rest because of weather conditions before our visitors Bristol scored 14 points to our 6 and another loss at home the following week when New Brighton notched up 29 points to Richmond's 3. Away to London Scottish, another loss recorded by 6-18 and away again at Kingsholm, Gloucester gave Richmond best by a single point at 16-15, but a home match versus Moseley meant we were losers 12-16. On to the West Country for a Good Friday game at Falmouth where the pack did the business and we won 22-3 - but the next day all points were scored by penalty goals and resulted in Camborne registering a 12-6 victory. High jinks on Easter Sunday meant that Penryn "thrashed" Richmond 6-3 on the Monday.

Back to The Athletic Ground for three home matches producing a loss against Neath 11-19 and two wins, over Rosslyn Park 22-11 and Streatham-Croydon 23-0.

Whilst the 1st XV were cavorting in Cornwall, the A XV departed for Germany where, in Osnabruck, they drew 3-3 with the Royal Regiment of Wales (both sides claimed to be depleted) and then an 11-8 victory over 1st Division, whose Captain, Peter Cheeseman, played in our 1st XV in 1963. They then returned two hundred miles to Osnabruck to score 12 points to nil against 2nd Division. The last challenge for a weary Richmond XV was the Tank Regiment which was repulsed 24-5.

A number of players featured prominently in the 1st XV and these were : James Aarvold, Stuart Almond, John Aylwin, Dicky Bateman, Ian Botes, Tony Bucknall, Geoff Clarke, Peter Cook, Phil Court, John Croker, Stuart Fleming, Ed Gould, Jonathan Harvey, Peter Hearn, Mike Humphreys, Nick Iceley, Tony Kitchin, Pat Lavery, Leigh Merrick, Chris Ralston, Ben Russell, Dave Sixton, Will Sleeman, Brian Strong and Dave Travis.

Life off the field was active with John Croker, Peter Cook, Robin Jolliffe, Jonathan Harvey, Stuart Fleming, Ed Gould, Tony Rowland, Bill Carnaby, Peter Jones, John Orrick, Andrew Barker, Brian Stoneman, Derek Osmond and John Aylwin all taking the plunge into matrimony, and David Travis broke the Commonwealth and UK record for the javelin.

To unite overseas friendships, Richmond entertained Chicago Lions and

Atlanta but, unfortunately, nobody recorded the scores or indeed against which XVs they played.

We were honoured by having Tony Bucknall selected for England five times and he also represented the Barbarians, London Counties and Eastern Counties. Roger Shackleton, the Cambridge Blue, was also an England cap whilst past captain Steve Smith captained India in an 11-9 victory over Ceylon. Other players who gained representative honours were Chris Ralston ((London Counties, Middlesex), Robin Whitcomb (S.W.Counties, Devon), Steve Richards (N.W.Counties, Yorkshire), Jonathan Harvey (Southern Counties and captaincy of Dorset and Wiltshire), Paddy Hinton (Cambridge University, Surrey), David Griffiths (Oxford University), Leigh Merrick (Combined Services, captaincy of Hampshire, Royal Navy), Graham Phillips (Combined Services, Royal Navy), David Atkinson (Dorset and Wiltshire), Andrew Barker and Tony Kitchin (Hertfordshire), Ian Botes and Geoff Clarke (Hampshire), Terry Brooke and Ben Russell (Surrey), John Croker (Middlesex), Ed Gould (Oxfordshire) and Andrew Peters (Sussex).

The biggest news coverage of the year concerned the position of Tremayne Rodd who, having played for London Scottish and won 14 caps between 1958 and 1965, decided, in his own words, "to get fit" after a lapse in the game. To this end, he commenced playing for the Richmond A XV, but injuries to other scrum halves meant that he was chosen for the 1st XV in February 1970 for the fixture versus New Brighton.

When that selection became public, our co-tenants London Scottish pronounced that Rodd was a professional and had forfeited his amateur status by covering the 1966 Lions Tour to Australia and New Zealand as a journalist. This was, at that time, his bone-fide occupation but the Scottish RFU regarded any action such as writing about rugby (even as an ex-player in 1966) as having crossed the line into professionalism.

Under the laws of the RFU, Tremayne remained eligible to play for Richmond and therefore the club received clearance to play Rodd. Unfortunately, an International Rugby Board ruling stipulated that all member unions should support each other's regulations on professionalism. The matter was highlighted by the fact that Richmond were due to play London Scottish on the Saturday after the New Brighton game and our co-tenants announced that they would cancel any fixture at whatever level in which Rodd appeared against them.

The Richmond Committee appreciated the difficulties and, after a meeting which reportedly lasted over five hours, selected Rodd for the fifth side - the only side not meeting London Scottish - who were due to play the Bank of England. However, the International Board's rule 4 was further bandied about and that stated that "No player who has transgressed the rules as to professionalism as laid down by any Union in membership with the Board, shall be eligible to take part in any game played under the jurisdiction of the Unions which constitute the Board".

The RFU, of course, was heavily involved, especially the then secretary Robin Prescott. Many frantic telephone calls resulted between him and the club but eventually it was felt necessary to issue the following statement: "in deference to the views of the London Scottish FC and the Scottish RFU and their interpretation of the Scottish by-laws on professionalism, Tremayne Rodd was not considered for any of the Richmond sides playing London Scottish on Saturday March 7th, nor will he be for any future game. Richmond wish to stress that they have followed this matter through with the Rugby Union since Rodd commenced playing in October and still consider him to be an amateur according to the English Rugby Union laws, but now have to abide by International agreements to an individual Board's decisions".

The above statement was backed by a release to the press that said "We are afraid Tremayne cannot play again. Over the next few days we shall of course be having further talks but at the moment he cannot play and cannot even serve on our committee or for that matter any other club as far as we can see. Whether there can be any appeal or reinstatement we do not know but we have no option but to comply with the rules".

Tremayne had been kept appraised of the situation and refused to talk to the media. He took the eventual outcome remarkably well, since he contested that he was still an amateur, recognising both the ruling and the fact that Richmond had to abide by it. He was educated at Downside and Royal Navy College Dartmouth, before serving in the Royal Navy from 1952 to 1962, and is now the third Baron Rennell of Rodd. As far as we know he has not played rugby since the above affair but enjoys Real Tennis. It is a pity that, at the time, we could not have had some real thinking from those in authority.

Sadly, in this year we also recorded the passing of one of legends of the club, R.H. (Horse) O'Brien

Chapter Two

The Seventies

1970/ 71

The Presidency and Secretaryship continued in the hands of Frank Bisgood and Alan Skeats respectively but, after all his years at the financial helm, John Black passed over the role of treasurer to Tony Vyvyan, our massive ex-centre who had previously played for Coventry and Warwickshire. Captain of the club was assumed by the former Cambridge Blue, Tony Kitchin, with coach Johnny Watterson aided by Ernie Preece and Colin Holman - a longstanding member teaching at Woodcote House School. The President had also become Chairman of the Executive Committee.

Saracens at Southgate was the first fixture of the season, resulting in a 6-6 draw but, after we won 11-9 at Rugby, the club suffered three successive losses - at Northampton 3-29, at Bedford 6-30 and at home to London Welsh 3-17. That was September, and October was no better showing a home win against Oxford University 8-3 but two more losses in that month going down at home twice - to Cambridge University 12-13 and Rosslyn Park 8-22.

A disastrous November with four losses - at home 0-26 versus Llanelli, at the Stoop where Harlequins won 9-3, at home again 9-13 to London Scottish and at Swansea going down 3-15.

December started in the same vein with London Irish defeating the club 17-5 at Sunbury, but we followed with two wins when both games at The Athletic Ground showed wins - of 44-9 versus St Mary's Hospital and 11-3 over Blackheath. A mixed January followed when defeat at home against the Army 8-11 preceded a win away at New Brighton 32-8, but was followed by two more losses - at home to Waterloo 3-6 and away at Coundon Road where Coventry sneaked a 8-6 win.

The Wasps lost to us 3-16 at Sudbury in February after which we drew 14-14 at the Rectory Field, Blackheath before two more losses ensued at Bristol 6-9 and against Gosforth 11-12 at home. Our away game with London Scottish in March repeated the loss sequence - we failed 6-9, then followed a win when Gloucester were the underdogs at our home game and lost 11-19.

The last four matches heightened the gloom with four successive away defeats - against Moseley 9-32, Bath 14-22, Neath 8-19 and Leicester 8-33.

Players who suffered in this poor season under Tony Kitchin were James Aarvold, Stuart Almond, Ian Botes, Hugh Braithwaite, David Buchanan, Phil

Davis, Stuart Fleming, Alan Harries, Paddy Hinton, Steve James, Pat Lavery, Elwyn Lloyd, Johnny (Remy) Martin, Leigh Merrick, Chris Ralston, Kevin Riordan, Mike Sale, Mike Smythe, Alistair Toms and John Walter.

The Vikings were in demi-sec mood in Epernay with a 19-0 win over Sélection Militaire Locale after the local newspaper described how they got into the "mode locale" with "champagne du petit dejeuner au coucher - et même aprés" so perhaps it was no surprise that the second game scoreline read R.C. Epérnay 8 Richmond Vikings 0.

It appears that the annual Richmond honours list was no longer produced so, regrettably, no detailed listings of representative honours exists but we can record with pride that Jeremy Janion and Chris Ralston were picked by England. Chris Ralston gained his first cap against Scotland before playing against the President's Overseas XV and toured the Far East in his country's jersey - where, incidentally, he came up against Tony Hallett, a future Richmond Chairman and President, playing for Hong Kong.

1971/ 2

Whilst the Presidency, Secretaryship and the post of Treasurer remained in the same hands, as did the chairmanship of the Executive, Steve (Heavy) James, late of Oxford University, became Captain with Colin Holman as Club Coach. Once again, results were somewhat mixed. The leading players to appear were James Aarvold, Hugh Braithwaite, Mark Brickell, David Buchanan, Tony Bucknall, John Deller, Mike Humphreys, Tony Kitchin, Pat Lavery, Derek Laybourne, Pat Liddiard, Humfrey Malins (currently MP for Woking), Mike Marshall, Stuart Maxwell, Leigh Merrick, Chris Ralston, Mike Sale, Brian Strong, Alistair Toms, Nigel Wilson and Dicky Woodall.

Again Saracens were the first fixture but, by the odd point, we lost at home, 11-12. The next two games as hosts saw wins over Wasps 16-13 and Northampton 15-12 before our visitors Bedford won 24-16. Old Deer Park in October meant a win for London Welsh over us 28-18 but at home Leicester were beaten 18-12 and then, in a quickly arranged fixture, our visitors from Australia, Eastern Suburbs of Sydney, triumphed 22-13. Oxford University were overcome 7-6 at Iffley Road and Gosforth away 13-9 but the month finished with a home loss to Rosslyn Park 10-24.

November began with a loss at Stradey against Llanelli 6-26 and four home games on the trot were up and down with a draw against Harlequins 4-4, a win against London Scottish 19-13, a defeat by Swansea 15-19 and a win over London Irish 37-14. The year ended with two losses away versus Rosslyn Park 4-19 and Blackheath 12-15.

January started with Wasps beating us 24-11 at Sudbury before the club strung together three away wins - against the Army 14-9, Cambridge University 29-6 and Waterloo 14-11. A fixture list showing five home games next gave results of 0-10 against Coventry, two wins 24-9 over Headingley and "The Club" Blackheath 30-22 before Bristol had the upper hand 15-10 then New Brighton went down to us 17-37 and, in March, Richmond lost 0-19 to London Scottish (away).

The last away game at Gloucester saw the home side win 17-0 whilst in the last four home games, Moseley scored 22 points to our 10 after which Bath were beaten 23-17, Percy Park went down 53-6 to us and finally Neath suffered at our hands 15-25.

There was only a fifty percent success rate on the Easter tour when, in the Pyrenees, St Giron were beaten 25-23 but Bagnères thrashed us 27-0.

Richmond were, of course, well represented at the RFU Centenary Banquet held at the Guildhall. This was attended by the eight existing founder clubs viz. Blackheath, Civil Service, Guy's Hospital, Harlequins, King's College, St Paul's School, Wellington College and ourselves, and a light meal was savoured comprising:

Turtle Soup	Madeira
Smoked Trout	Domaine de Vaumartin 1966
Roast Saddle of Lamb, Brussel Sprouts, Roast Potatoes	Chateau Beau-Site 1962
Rhum Ba-Ba filled with black cherries and cream	Port: Taylor's Vintage Reserve
Devils on horseback	Drambuie
Kummel Coffee	

The toast to the RFU was proposed by our own Sir John Megaw C.B.E, T.D. International honours were gained by J.P.A.G (the initials given to avoid mistaken identity) Janion and Chris Ralston for England (also played for London Counties) Recognition was also centred on other Richmond players who played against the All Blacks: Geoff Clarke and Rod Mulvey (New York Metropolitan Clubs); Tony Bucknall (London Counties); Stuart Maxwell - the only Englishman to score two tries against them (N.W.Counties); Humfrey Malins and Mike Marshall (Southern Counties); Leigh Merrick, Phil Davies and Graham Phillips (who also turned out for Cambridge University against the New Zealanders) - all Combined Services and Jonathan Dickins (Cambridge University). In his first game for the Barbarians, Phil Davies scored a brace of tries and Chris Ralston toured South Africa with England.

On a very sad note, the passing was recorded of the inimitable "Nim" Hall who joined Richmond in 1949/50, having already captained England. He was capped seventeen times over a span of nine years and was our captain in 1953.

1972/3

As fully recorded in the national press, Murray Judd, a fearsome Richmond prop and co-founder of the Heavies, became President, the youngest of any senior club, with Tom Rider taking Chairmanship of the Executive Committee whilst Alan Skeats, Tony Vyvyan and Steve James remained in their posts of Secretary, Treasurer and Captain, as did Club Coach Colin Holman.

Not a very good season with sixteen wins, one draw and sixteen losses. It started off reasonably in September with victories - Cambridge City (home) 59-4 and Wasps 43 - 17 (away), a draw at Franklin's Gardens against Northampton 21-21 and another win at Goldington Road where our score over Bedford was 18-16. We then went to Roehampton where we lost 10-15 to Rosslyn Park after which defeats were suffered at home to London Welsh 0-16 and at Welford Road when Leicester won by a massive 44-7.

A pick up for four matches which resulted in victories. The first three at home against Oxford University 10-6, Cambridge University 18-7, two of whose players, Charlie Goodall and Jonathan Dickens, were later to join Richmond, Llanelli 18-9 a week after they had beaten the All Blacks with virtually the same team and Harlequins 9-8. The pick up did not last because Richmond then suffered five defeats in a row - versus London Scottish at home 12-22, Swansea away 4-10 at St Helens, London Irish away 0-4, Rosslyn Park 13-36 and Blackheath 22-24, both at The Athletic Ground. The last matches in December produced a home win against Harlequins 22-0 but an away loss 18-25 to Coventry.

The first matches of 1973 gave us two home wins - over Wasps 9-3 and Saracens 12-9 but, as in so many seasons, it was on and off again with a loss away at Gosforth 3-18, two wins over Waterloo 48-6 (played at Old Deer Park) and Headingley away 25-21 before two slumps versus Blackheath 9-13 and Bristol 6-32, both games also away.

A win at the end of February at home over London Irish was 18-4 but then we travelled to an away game at London Scottish and came away empty-handed 15-29. The home match with Gloucester was clinched 29-21, then followed another three defeats at the hands of Moseley at The Reddings 9-10, at Bath 12-31, and at Saracens in Southgate 17-42.

Mercifully, the season ended in April with a victory at Neath at The Knoll

17-9 and Percy Park at home went down to Richmond 3-22. Another Easter tour to France brought victories over St Giron 23-16 and Bagnères 23-19.

Under Steve James the main players involved were David Buchanan, Phil Davies, Bill Hadman, Peter Hearn, Paddy Hinton, Peter Howland, Jeremy Janion, Tony Kitchin, Pat Lavery, Pat Liddiard, Stuart Maxwell, Leigh Merrick, Chris Ralston, Ben Russell, Derek Ryan, Mike Sale, Roger Steth, Brian Strong, Robin Whitcomb and Nigel Wilson. Caps for England were won by Jeremy Janion and Chris Ralston.

1973/74

All four offices of President, Secretary, Treasurer, Chairman of Executive and Club Coach remained unchanged but a new Captain appeared in Anthony Lance Bucknall, another Oxford Blue of distinction.

Under Tony's captaincy the following players played the most times for the 1st XV: Lynn Adams, Robin Bell, Neil Boult, Mike Humphreys, Steve James, Jeremy Janion, Pat Lavery, Bob McGrath, Stuart Maxwell, Chris Ralston, Phil Reid, Ben Russell, Pat Slattery, Brian Strong, David Whibley and Nigel Wilson.

Unfortunately, another "iffish" season - "if only" in so many games. A bright start with an away game at Oxford with the scoreline to us 32-13 followed by a defeat of Wasps at home 14-3 and the next day we entertained Chicago but the scoreline is not known. Northampton travelled to us and won 26-10 after which, still at home, Richmond defeated Bedford 22-6 followed by a loss to Rosslyn Park 7-14.

In October, London Welsh were beaten 26-3 away, Leicester won on our ground 16-0 and then in Oxford we beat the University 17-16 before going to Grange Road and letting Cambridge University register a 13-6 victory. Knock-out competitions had now come into being with the John Player Cup and, in the first round, we put out Metropolitan Police 21-13. In November the results were Llanelli away an 18-40 loss, Harlequins at home a win by 20-6, a defeat by London Scottish away 13-18 and a victory over Swansea here in Richmond by 16-4.

December started with a home match, the opponents being London Irish and we won 8-6. At Roehampton the following week Rosslyn Park scored 21 to our 18 points. At Blackheath we won 13-9 with two more wins following - at Harlequins 23-16 and home to Coventry 18-9.

At the start of the New Year at Sudbury, Wasps beat us 4-3 and then there was a draw away with Saracens 15-15 before a home cup tie against Gosforth saw a 25-19 victory. At Blundellsands, Waterloo saw Richmond off 10-6 and, in the first week of February, Headingley came to us and went away winners 26-20.

Then came the next round of the John Player Cup and, in a thrilling match as the first of a double-header, (London Scottish were at home to Northampton) we saw off Bristol in the final minutes by 16-14 after an amazing forty yards burst for a try by Phil (Filthy) Reid. London Irish were beaten 9-7 away but then followed three defeats at The Athletic Ground by St Luke's College 3-28, London Scottish in the next round of the John Player Cup 0-7 and Moseley 9-18.

That, thankfully, was the last loss as we finished the season with a 14-14 draw with Bath at home; a victory at Thornton Heath over Streatham-Croydon 22-9 and another at home over Neath 49-15 and 40-7 against New Brighton when they travelled south. Another big honour for the club as Chris Ralston went on the all-conquering British Lions Tour of South Africa. A few weeks after the tour the following scene took place:

Subject:	Chris Ralston
Scene:	The London Office of a well-known firm of Accountants
Participants:	The two Senior Partners (who know nothing about Rugby) and Chris Ralston (who does). The official meeting has finished and Chris has graciously accepted a large cigar.
Accountant:	(with stutter and seeing Chris's tanned face) "b-b-been away recently?"
Chris:	"Yes" (his usual flowing conversational style)
Accountant:	(trying desperately to make conversation) "Where t-t-to?"
Chris:	"South Africa"
Accountant:	(moment of inspiration) "Whilst there, did you see anything of the B-B-British Lions?"
Chris:	"Only when I wasn't playing for them" !

1974/5

Murray Judd, Alan Skeats, Tony Vyvyan and Tom Rider remained in their respective offices but the Captaincy passed to Chris (Lurch) Ralston, with Ken Morley (Windsor Grammar School) as Club Coach and, apart from a dire start to 1975, the results were very good, culminating in the club being awarded the Sunday Telegraph Merit Pennant.

Early season starts in the West Country saw off Exeter 15-9 and Teignmouth 47-17 before returning home to score 25 points to Streatham-Croydon's 3. However, stiffer opposition registered a loss at Wasps 16-22 but we recovered to win 10-3 over Northampton at Franklin's Gardens. Another four victories were to follow at Bedford 15-9, home over London Welsh 15-3, away at Leicester 16-9 and 38-9 over our visitors Oxford University. Two losses both at home versus Cambridge University 8-16 and Llanelli 3-6 were recorded before Richmond strung together eight victories with, firstly, a win over Harlequins 24-6 away. This was followed by London Scottish (home) 20-3, away at Swansea 13-9 and away at Roehampton 16-10 over Rosslyn Park, before in December away to London Irish 15-12 and a similar score a week later at home to Rosslyn Park and again at home over Blackheath 14-6 before finishing the year with a John Player Cup game at Thornton Heath where we ran out winners against Streatham-Croydon 10-3.

Disaster at the start of 1975 when five losses in a row were recorded, two at home - against Wasps (19-9) and Saracens also made the same score against us, then away at Gosforth, Richmond went down 12-23 followed by a home defeat by Waterloo 6-17 and then home club Headingley won 10-0.

We then took on Morley in the knockout competition and won 14-6 at home. We then went away to the Memorial Ground and, in the evening, beat Bristol 12-7. Returning home there was a 9-9 draw with London Irish before journeying to London Scottish where we won again 15-14. An interesting fixture a week later when Richmond entertained a Spanish Combination XV and won 10-4, and then came a win at the Recreation Ground 10-9 over Bath. The two final matches achieved a 17-4 victory at Neath but ended on a dull note going down 4-13 to Notts at Beeston.

The leading players who served under Chris Ralston were Colin Ashby, Neil Boult, Tony Bucknall, R.J. 'Jumbo' Edwards, Peter Hearn, Brian Hegarty, Brian Hester, Mike Humphreys, Steve James, Jeremy Janion, Stuart Maxwell, Alan Mort, Terry O'Hanlon, Rick Pearson, Gerry Redmond, Martin Ridley, Roger Shackleton, Brian Strong, Glen Waugh and Dave Whibley.

Notably, David Whibley scored 214 points, the highest total ever recorded by a Richmond player in a single season whilst Jeremy Janion and Chris Ralston were again honoured by England.

1975/6

Murray Judd who assumed Chairmanship of the Executive gave way to John Riley as President, Alan Skeats and Tony Vyvyan continued as Secretary and Treasurer. Chris Ralston and Ken Morley stood in for a second term as Captain and Club Coach respectively, and we started off with no losses until October.

The season begun with a short tour of the West Country and two wins 19-7 at Torquay and 26-0 against Bridgewater and Albion then away again to Brigstock Road where the score was 15-3 over Streatham-Croydon. The first home game resulted in a 15-15 draw with Wasps, then Northampton visited us and lost 6-13 followed by Bedford at The Athletic Ground and the score was 10-0 in Richmond's favour.

October arrived and we departed from the John Player Cup by losing away to London Welsh 6-21, however we recovered to beat Leicester 20-14 at home and Oxford University 30-16 away. Then came a string of three losses - away to Cambridge University 22-34, at Stradey Park 6-27 to Llanelli and 9-14 against Harlequins, our visitors.

A home recovery when we beat London Scottish 22-7 but then another three defeats, all at home, when we lost to Swansea 14-13, Rosslyn Park 10-3 and London Irish 22-19 before wins were gained over Rosslyn Park 27-14 at Roehampton and Blackheath 15-9 at the Rectory Field. The Christmas match at Twickenham gave Harlequins an easy victory 40-9 whilst, on the last day of the year, touring side Le Zebre from South Africa were beaten 38-24.

1976 brought a mixed bag of results with two wins at home over Wasps 9-6 and at Southgate against Saracens 21-9 before Gosforth visited us and won 21-6. At Blundellsands, a win was recorded over Waterloo 16-6 and, after the wintry conditions stopped a home match at Coventry, three Athletic Ground games gave wins over Headingley 13-12 and Blackheath 22-12 but a loss to Bristol 0-12.

London Irish were beaten 25-14 away and London Scottish 13-7 (away) but a visit to Gloucester meant a 4-17 defeat and then Moseley scored 29 points to our 12 at The Athletic Ground. The last three games were all at home when we beat Bath 8-6, lost to Neath 6-29 and won against Nottingham 20-13.

This season saw the following players appear most times for Richmond under Chris Ralston namely Colin Ashby, Tony Boddy, Tony Bucknall, Phil Davies, Jonathan Dickins, Willie Dickinson, Gary Greenwood, Peter Hearn, Brian Hester, Steve James, Jeremy Janion, Pat Lavery, Paul Morris, Alan Mort, Peter Philp, Roger Shackleton, Neil Vinter and David Whibley.

1976/7

John Riley and Alan Skeats were still in office as President and Secretary respectively whilst the post of Treasurer went to Jeremy Janion and Roger Shackleton became Captain, assisted by Club Coach Ken Morley. Murray Judd remained as Chairman of the Executive Committee, in a season in which the R.F.U. first allowed the use of replacements.

Again, the West Country was the start of the season's campaign the first fixture being at Beacon Park where Plymouth Albion were overcome 18-9 and a similar score, 18-7, recorded our win at Brixham. A final tour match saw a 23-6 result in our favour at Taunton Road over Bridgewater and Albion. Also in September, Streatham-Croydon visited us and lost 0-18 when the replacement law was utilised and Terry O'Hanlon was the first for Richmond. At Sudbury, Wasps won 14-9 before two away matches gave us victory at Franklin's Gardens against Northampton 15-10, but we then lost 16-30 in the match at Goldington Road, Bedford.

Unfortunately, a normal sort of "win some, lose some" Richmond season continued. October recorded losses against London Welsh 6-9 (home) and 12-24 at Leicester then a win of 26-12 over Oxford University at home before, at Grange Road, Cambridge outscored us 17-10 and then Rosslyn Park at home went down to us 7-25.

November produced two losses - 7-16 at home to Llanelli and 9-13 to Harlequins at Twickenham before an away journey to London Scottish gave Richmond a 17-3 win and, in another away game at St Helens, Swansea won 20-12. Torquay Athletic hosted us in December and we won 21-11 before weather interfered with our Rosslyn Park fixture and the year ended in triumph over Blackheath at home 15-6.

New Year's Day and we had a 12-0 win over Wasps, then Saracens visited us and it was a 26-16 win for Richmond. Then snow saw the cancellation of the match at New Ground, Gosforth, before Waterloo travelling to us record-ed a 24-14 victory. A visit to Coundon Road gave Richmond the edge 18-16 over Coventry. A disastrous February with Headingley winning at home 4-3, Saracens won at Southgate 15-7, Bristol at the Memorial Ground beat Richmond 23-6 and home side London Irish edged it 16-15 at Sunbury.

London Scottish playing away scored 22 points to our 18 after which the journey to Blackheath gave us a 19-13 win. Other March results were failures at Moseley 0-9, at Bath 4-25 then in April at the Knoll, Neath outscored us 10-7 before the final fixture at Ireland Avenue produced a 16-16 draw with Nottingham.

Under Roger Shackleton, the season's photograph shows these players:

Colin Ashby, Jeff Bannister, Adrian Barnes, Tony Bucknall, Steve Curran, Phil Davies. Jonathan Dickins, Willie Dickinson, Neil Dobson, Gary Greenwood, Michael Hess, Malcolm Hickey, Jeremy Janion, Alan Mansfield, Alan Mort, Terry O'Hanlon, Rick Pearson, Peter Philip, Chris Pritchard, Ian Ray, Chris Ralston, Alf Shortland, Neil Vinter, David Whibley and John Yeomans.

1977/8

President, Secretary, Chairman of the Executive and Captain were still John Riley, Alan Skeats, Murray Judd and Roger Shackleton respectively but, although originally nominated, Jeremy Janion gave way to David (Tripper) Allen, a scrum-half and one of the early Heavies Captains, as Treasurer. On the coaching side, a Panel was set up comprising Ken Morley, Colin Holman, Leigh Merrick, (our former back row player and sailor) and Nigel Wilson, our old sevens star.

A somewhat better season for the club with fifteen wins, ten losses and one draw mainly using the following players: Colin Ashby, Steve Curran, Martin Edwards, Michael Hess, Brian Hester, W.G.Boyd Morrison III, Alan Mort, Rick Pearson, Nick Preston, Chris Pritchard, Chris Ralston, David Rollitt, Chris Sharpe, Alf Shortland, David Whibley and Martin Wood.

Another West Country start to the season although the first game was in Wales at Parc Di Owen where Whitland were beaten 27-7. We then travelled to Plymouth when the home side inflicted an 18-7 defeat on us, but the next day victory was ours at Torquay by 12-6.

Back at The Athletic Ground for three home games, the first two being wins 6-4 over Wasps and 9-6 over Northampton but then Bedford ran in winners 12-11 after which we remained scoreless at Old Deer Park when London Welsh notched up 15 points. Leicester came to Richmond and went back losers 6-9, then visits to the universities gave us wins of 26-3 at Oxford and 20-13 at Cambridge, but Rosslyn Park stopped our run holding us to a 6-6 draw at Richmond.

November was a poor month, starting with defeat at Llanelli 8-23, a home win against Harlequins 11-0, followed by two home losses to London Scottish 9-16 and Swansea 7-19. December was not too good either; starting with our visitors London Irish winning 6-3, although victories were recorded in away matches at Rosslyn Park 13-12 and Blackheath 35-7, before Harlequins at Twickenham outscored us 43-15 and, at The Athletic Ground, Wilmslow won 7-6.

The inception of the John Player Cup in January meant an away game with Wasps and, although the result was an even 9-9, we were adjudged the losers. The next week, again in North London, we outpointed Saracens 10-3

RICHMOND FOOTBALL CLUB

Our History in Pictures
Section One

This section covers the period from 1961 to 1989. Alas, the destruction of the Long Bar during the 'professional' era led to the loss of many team photos, especially from the 1970s/80s

Who better to introduce this section than Chris Ralston - British Lions, England, Barbarians, London Counties, Middlesex and Richmond.

Centenary Match Saturday 2nd September 1961
Richmond v Major Gen. R.G.B. Hobb's International XV

Back: J.M. Williams, J.P. Horrocks-Taylor, C.R. Segal, A.J.F. O'Reilly, P.F.G. Charteris, G.J. Bendon, G. Windsor-Lewis, R.W.D. Marques, B.M. Stoneman, G.W. Payne, P. Thoming, J.A.P. Shackleton, G.W. Fox, J. Leleu, M.P. Weston, Gwynne Walters (Referee), F.H. Bisgood (Hon.Sec)

Middle: S.R. Smith, A.R. Smith, M.E. Wates, Major Gen. R.G.S. Hobbs (President R.F.U.), K.J.F. Scotland (Capt.), W.C.O. Munks (Capt.), C.R. Hopwood (President R.F.C.), I.H.P. Laughland, P.H. Ryan, R.P. Boggon

Front: P.R. Burns, J.A.S. Wackett, R.J. Moyle, J.E. Williams, M.E. Reuben, N.S. Bruce, P.G.R. Orr, W.G.D. Morgan

Richmond 1st XV 1961-2

F.H. Bisgood (Hon Sec), F.T.A. Hole, C.R. Segal, J.E. Aves, B.M. Stoneman, C.K. Pearce, F.E.R. Butler, A.R. Fitch, D.R. Proud, P.C.R. Orr

P.R. Burns, G. Windsor-Lewis, S.R. Smith, W.G.O. Munks (Capt), M.E. Wates, G.W. Fox, P.F.G. Charteris

A.A. Holmes,   B.D. Dykes

Richmond 1st XV 1962-3

F.W. Lovell (Hon Sec), P.C.R. Orr, J.A. Collingwood, B.M. Stoneman, S.J. Good, P.R. Burns, W.M.J. Pope, P. Thorning, C.M. Judd (Team Sec)

F.T.A. Hole, A.B. Vyvyan, C.R. Hopwood (President), G. Windsor-Lewis, S.R. Smith, F.E.R. Butler, G.W. Fox

R.J.W. Poole, P.W. Cook, D.M. Kilminster, J.A. Boyd-Smith, A.R. Pitch

Richmond 1st XV 1963-4

N.B. Pinnington (Hon Sec), D.A. Webster, C.J. Allan, J.A. Collingwood, M.P. Elphick, K.R. Ebenezer, E.W. Preece, P.R. Burns, W.G. Campbell, P.C.R. Orr, C.M. Judd (Team Sec)

F.T.A. Hole, F.E.R. Butler, M.E. Wales, S.R. Smith, F. Mennin (President), P.F.G. Charteris, B.M. Stoneman, P. Thorning

D. Hawkes,   P.W. Cook

Richmond1st XV 1964-5

P.W. Cook, T. Jones, B.T.N. Jones, R.D.F. Robins

N.B. Pinnington (Hon-Sec), M.J. Lee, K.R. Ebenezer, P. Thorning, B.D. Richards, C.W. Ralston, I. Brown, C.J. Allan, C.M. Judd (Team Sec)

D.A. Webster, P.R. Burns, S.R. Smith (Captain), F. Mennim (President), M.E. Wates, B.M. Stoneman, F.E.R. Butler

Richmond 1st XV 1965-6

I.B. Moffatt, I. Brown, R. Bruce, E.W. Preece, K.R. Ebenezer, C.W. Ralston, A. Blake, R.D.F. Robins, J.M. Alwin, C.M. Judd

P.W. Cook, J.A. Collingwood, P.F.G. Charteris, F.T.A. Hole (Captain), B.M. Stoneman, S.B. Richard, H.G. Waller

A.C. Davies, P.W. Raymond,   R.H. Bateman, I. Palmer-Lewis

Richmond 1st XV 1966-7

T.S. Rider (President), T.P. Bedford, W.G. Hadman, T.J. Brooke, J.R.W. Harvey, R.P.K. Whitcomb, L.G. Cormack, C.W. Ralston, I.B. Moffatt, T.C. Jones, C.M. Judd (linesman)

H.G. Waller, R.L.K. Joliff, S.B. Richards, B.M. Stoneman (Captain), R.H. Bateman, PW. Cook

Richmond 1st XV 1967-8

C.M. Judd (linesman), R.F.K. Whitcomb, A. Blake, W.G. Hadman, J.R.W. Harvey, C.W. Ralston, E.W. Preece, F.J.R. Craig, R.S. Fleming, A. Page (Sec)

R.H. Bateman, T.P. Bedford, B.M. Stoneman, L.G. Cormack (Captain), T.S. Rider (President), C.J. Allan, T.J. Brooke, C.W. Ball, J.P. Waterson (Coach)

D.G. Hawkes, H.G. Waller, M.K. Davis

Richmond 1st XV 1968-9

C.P. Simpson, P.A. Kitchen, R.S. Fleming, C.W. Ralston, J.R.W. Harvey, A. Blake, A.L. Bucknall, I.H.C. Botes, B.L. Lee, P. Hearn, C.F. Waterman, P.M. Baron, N. Hook, J.A. Boyd-Smith

P.H.D. Lavery, J.M. Aylwin, C.J. Allan, D.G. Hawkes, J.P. Waterson, E.W. Preece (Captain), T.S. Rider (President), R.H. Bateman, O.C.A. Bell, N.C.G. Wilson, J.R. Croker, A. Page

RICHMOND

Full Back	D. WHIBLEY	16
Right Wing	R. M. S. WOODALL	15
Right Centre	J. JANION	14
Left Centre	G. F. CLARKE	12
Left Wing	N. R. BOULT	11
Outside Half	P. M. D. LAVERY	10
Inside Half	N. J. C. WILSON	9
Prop	P. J. SLATTERY	1
Hooker	B. RUSSELL	2
Prop	D. F. BUCHANAN	3
Lock	S. J. V. JAMES	4
Lock	C. W. RALSTON	5
Wing Forward	P. HEARN	6
No. 8	L. C. P. MERRICK	8
Wing Forward	A. L. BUCKNALL	7

LLANELLI

Colours - Scarlet

15	ROGER DAVIES	Cefnwr
14	JOHN WILLIAMS	Asgell Dde
13	ROY BERGIERS	Canolwr De
12	RAYMOND GRAVELLE	Canolwr Chwith
11	ANDY HILL	Asgell Chwith
10	PHIL BENNETT	Maswr
9	SELWYN WILLIAMS	Mewnwr
1	TONY CROCKER	Y Rheng Flaen
2	ROY THOMAS	Bachwr
3	CHRIS CHARLES	Y Rheng Flaen
4	DEREK QUINNELL	Clo
5	JEF PYLES	Clo
6	TOM DAVID	Blaenasgell
8	HEFIN JENKINS	Wythwr
7	ALAN JAMES	Blaenasgell

Rheolwr Referee: Mr. D. A. BIDDER, Swansea

Llanelli won this particular encounter 40-18. Richmond won 18-9 the season before, a week after Llanelli had defeated the All-Blacks with a virtually identical team.

Players of the 70s

Jeremy Janion

Nigel Gillingham

Tony Bucknall

Steve James/Brian Strong

Players of the 70s

Alan Mort

Phil Davies

Roger Shackleton

David Buchanan et al

Players of the 70s

Chris Ralston

Pat Liddiard

Stuart Maxwell

Pat Lavery

Sevens Achievements

Richmond has one of the best sevens records of any club in the country - a reputation based mainly on a 'golden age' between 1974 and 1983 when Richmond reached the Finals of the Middlesex Sevens no less than seven times, winning the trophy on six occasions.

1974 Nigel Wilson

1975 Pat Lavery

1980 Terry O'Hanlon

7s Action

Try imminent...

Try imminent...

The Richmond machine glides smoothly into action...

Richmond FC, Winners Middlesex 7s, RFU Twickenham, 1974

N.Sanson (Referee), B. Hadman, N. Boult, A. Bucknall, P. Hearn

S. Maxwell, N. Wilson (Captain), P. Lavery

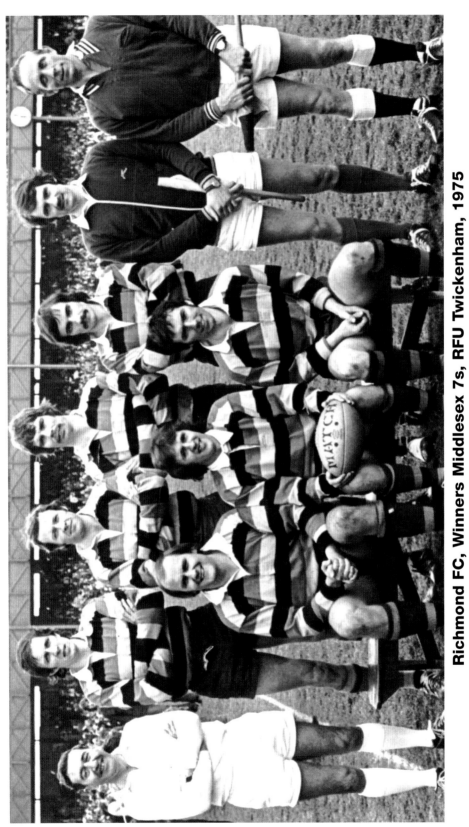

Richmond FC, Winners Middlesex 7s, RFU Twickenham, 1975

D.Spyer (Referee), N.Bolt, S.Maxwell, B.Hadman, T.O'Hanlon, N.Sanson, J. Johnston, (Touch Judges)

A.Bucknall, P.Lavery (Captain), P.Hearn

Richmond FC, Winners Middlesex 7s, RFU Twickenham, 1977

Touch Judge, N. Vinter, N. Dobson, C. Yeomans, N. Sanson, (Touch Judge), M. Stobart, J. Tring, (Referee)

T.O'Hanlon, A. Mort, R. Shackleton (Captain), J. Janion

Richmond FC, Winners Middlesex 7s, RFU Twickenham, 1979

G. Greenwood, R.Pearson, N. Mallett, N. Preston, M. Stobart, R.Mayle,

P. Williams, R. Shackleton, (Captain), I. Ray, T. O'Hanlon

Richmond FC, Winners Middlesex 7s, RFU Twickenham, 1980

R.C. Quittenton (Referee), R.Shackleton, A. Barnes, N. Dobson, N. Preston, J. Smith, M. Stobart

N. Vinter, C. Yeomans, T. O'Hanlon (Captain), I. Ray, C. Lambert

Richmond FC, Winners Gala Centenary 7s, 1984

Top: C. Holman (Management), S. Jackson, G. Prichenfried, J. Lamb, C. Vyvyan

Bottom: J. Fenton, I. Ray (Captain), J. Dyson, M. Conner, P. Lavery (Coach)

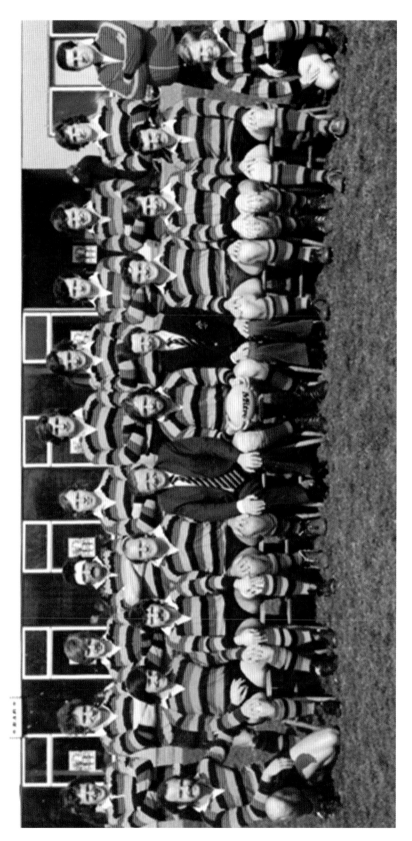

Richmond 1st XV 1975/6

P. Lavery, W. Dickinson, N. Vinter, B. Hester, P. Morris, J. Dickins, G. Greenwood, P. Davies, T. Boddy, R. McGrath, G. Tardiff (1st XV Sec)

R. Shackleton, A. Mort, D. Whibley, A. Bucknall, J. Riley (President), C. Ralston (Captain), A. Skeats (Secretary), S. James

J. Janion, P. Hearn, P. Philp

A.V.H.
SKEATS
touch
judge

A.
NEARY
Broughton
Park & England

M.I.
STOBART
t/secty.

A.J.
SHORTLAND

G. GREENWOOD

W.J.
McBRIDE
Ballymena & Ireland

G.
WOOD
London
Scottish

P.J.
HARDING

N.J.
PRESTON

S.
HUGHES

D.
TRICK

R. GORDON (London Scottish)

C.J.
MATTEY

P.
WARFIELD
Bath

M. PYRGOS

A.
RIPLEY
Rosslyn Park & England

R.
WARFIELD
Rosslyn Park
& England

R.D.F.
ROBINS

D.M.
ROLLITT
Richmond
& England

C.
RALSTON
Rosslyn Park

B.C.
HESTER

A.
OLD
Sheffield
& England

G. M.
de P. TARDIF
touch judge

J.P.
PICKIN

N.
SANSOM
referee

P.
WINDER

F.
COTTON

J.A.
CASTLE
Sale &
Secretary

C.W.
RALSTON
Richmond
& England

R.
EDWARDS

J.F.
STOY
President

M.A.H.
HESS
Captain

K.
KENNEDY
London Irish
& Ireland

P.
GIBSON

A.D.
MORT

Sale &
England

C.W.
LAMBERT

L.
BARLOW
Rosslyn Park

I.
RAY

S.
SMITH
Sale & England

C.J.
PRITCHARD

N.J.
VINTER

I. R.
SHACKLETON

Richmond 1st XV 1982-3

R. Hurst, P. Lavery, J. Thorn, A. Hamilton, K. Bassom, C. Heather, L. Williams, I. Warren, M.R. Slagter, M.A.H. Hess, P. Williams, N. Whitehead, J. Smith, P. Hearn, M.I. Stobart,

N.J. Vinter, J. Probyn, S. Pennock, N. Preston, A.V.H. Skeats (President), C.H. Sharpe (Captain), D.F. Whibley, S. Kelly, C. Green

Touring Action

1972 Uganda 12 - Richmond 55 (a match President Amin failed to attend)

1972 Tanzania 0 - Richmond 56 (Played in Dar-es-Salaam)

East Africa Tour 1972, Nondescripts 9 Richmond 34

Back: B. Slatter, K. Granger-Brown, P. Moore, M. Evans, P. Hearn, H. Mallins, A. Rees, R Vallings, R. Jones

Centre: J. Holman, C. Trapman, B. Strong, P. Evans, M. Humphreys, G. Davies, J. Arnold, C. Field, P. Liddiard, R. Sexton, A. Skeats (Manager), J. Powell-Rees (Referee)

Front: P. Plumbe, W. Campbell, P. Orr, S. James, C.M. Judd (President Richmond FC), E.A. Bristow Nondescripts FC), B. Granville-Ross, A. Bucknall, G. Wright, L. Merrick

Sitting Front: J. Martin, I. Carruthers, J. Deller, C. Wear

RICHMOND TOUR OF EAST AFRICA – MAY 1963

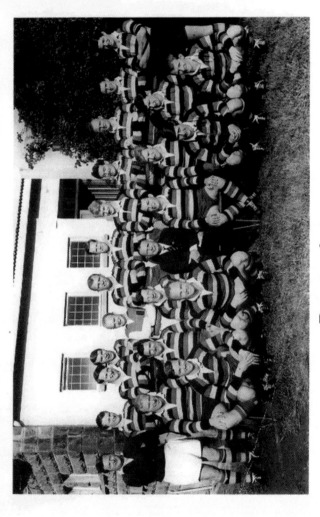

REUNION LUNCH

THE ROYAL THAMES YACHT CLUB – TUESDAY 8TH NOVEMBER 2005

Remarkably, 15 of the original party of 22 attended the 42½ year anniversary of the first club tour outside Europe by any club side.

Attendees: Bobby Burns, Robin Butler, Paul Charteris, Peter Cook, David Froud, Tony Hole, Murray Judd, Eric Lipscombe, Pat Orr, Ian Palmer-Lewis, Mike Pope, Ernie Preece, Stephen Smith, Tony Vyvyan and Geoffrey Windsor-Lewis. Absent: Dai Hawkes and Peter Thorning.

Absent Friends: Peter Cheeseman, Fruity Fox, Charles Hopwood (President), Bill Munks and Brian Stoneman.

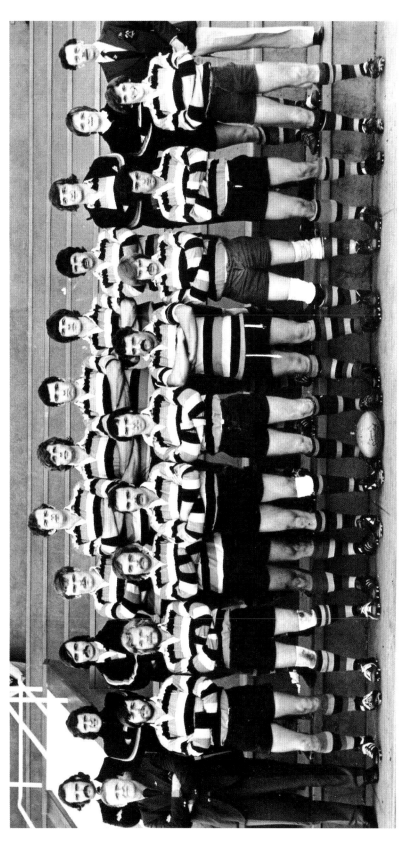

Richmond FC 1976 Tour to South Africa

R. Shackleton, P. Lavery, T. O'Hanlon, P. Williams, M. Humphreys, J. Dickins, M. Hess, R. Pearson, D. Whibley, G. Greenwood, C. Ashby, A. Skeats (Tour Manager)

John Riley (President), A. Mort, P.Philp, M. Brickell, I. Ray, P. Hearn, B. Hester, N. Vinter, A.Barns, R.McGrath

Richmond Heavies Tour of South Africa 1979

Back Row: Rob Brooks, P. Key, D. Rousso, Charlie Yeomans

3rd Row: Hugh Whitton, John Yeomans, Ray Hill, Tony Boyd-Smith, Roddy Adams, Tony Stansfield, D. Williams III, D. James, Mike Morgan

2nd Row: Tripper Allen, Tony Kent, Steve James, Charles Evans, Polly Rawlings, Paul Morris, James Aarvold, Chiz Chisnell, R. Vallings, B. Marsham

Seated: Phil Reid, Rob Robins, Brian Kirwan, Tony Bucknall (Coach), Dave Buchanan (Captain), Mike Humphries, Spike Espey (Manager), Ian Botes, Bob Blaney

Richmond Football Club Tour to Australia & Fiji, 1983

S.A.A. Pennock, N.J. Vinter, J.C. Wright, S.J. Factor, R.A. Osbourne, M.R. Conner, C.W. Mackaness, J.L. Thom, R.G. Beaumont

P.M. Williams, J.E. Fenton, R. Holman, B.P. Crawshaw, W.M. Reichwald, N.A. Whitehead, M.R. Catt, H.J. Stevenson, D.L. Goodwin, A. Janes, T.A. Evans

S.S. Burling, R.J. Edwards, D.F. Whibley (Assistant Manager), A.V.H. Skeats (President), M.A.H. Hess (Captain), R.D. Adams (Manager), C.H. Sharpe, M.R. Slagter, N.J. Preston, L.G. Williams

Richmond F.C. 125th Anniversary Tour, Paraguay & Brazil, July 1986

Back Row: G. Beaumont, M. Oliveira, J. McKenzie, S. Faktor, D. Sole, B. Hester (Coach), W. Bushell, M. Conner, M. Roper, J. Wright, T. Martineau

Middle Row: R. Hurst (Physio), P. Williams, M. Jones, C. Mackaness, R. Edwards, M. James, S. Attfield, N. Preston, D. Kenningham, C. Mills, J. Turner, M. Drain, D. Roxburgh, P. Southern

Front Row: R. Holman, S. Pennock, D. Goodwin, M. Slagter, J. Cullen (Vice Captain), A. Hampel (Captain), A. Skeats (Immediate Past President), President Brazillian RFU, R. Adams (Manager), J. Fenton, S. Alum before we lost 10-26 to Gosforth on home soil.

Instead of playing Waterloo away, we entertained Birmingham at home, the result 18-6 to us. Then Headingley came down and won 3-0. Weather stopped the next two games (home) with Blackheath and Bristol and, instead of going to London Irish, the Royal Navy were welcomed - result 28-12 to Richmond. Our co-tenants London Scottish were beaten 31-9 (away) and the Army at Aldershot fell to us 3-16. Four home matches resulted with wins over Moseley 13-10 and Neath 12-6, and then Bath had much the better of the game 38-9 with a last victory 25-13 against Nottingham.

On 1st May 1978 a special match was arranged to honour the memory of Brian Strong who, whilst working in North Africa, had holidayed in Spain where he bought a model airplane kit to construct. Upon his return to Algeria, he tried to soften the adhesive supplied under the shower whilst he was in it - tragically the fumes this caused overcame him and he died.

The club XV for this occasion comprised David Whibley, Alan Mort, Mike Edwards, Roger Shackleton, W.G Boyd Morrison III, Nick Preston, Chris Pritchard, Alfie Shortland, Neil Vinter, Willie Dickinson, Michael Hess, Chris Ralston, Rick Pearson, Dave Rollitt and Chris Sharpe.

Such was the esteem in which Brian was held that the following leading players appeared for the opposition, many of them with international caps to their names: Bob Hillier (England); Derek Wyatt (England), R. McGibbon (Ireland), Dave Croydon, Stuart Maxwell; Clive Rees, Ron Wilson (Scotland), John Fraser, Phil Keith-Roach, G. Lloyd-Roberts, Neil Mantell, Steve James, John Hill, Andy Ripley
and Tony Bucknall (England) and the match was refereed by George Walker.

The result is unimportant but a tribute was paid and Brian's influence on the game is typified by my programme notes on the day - "The diversity of rugby throughout the world produces an amazing cross-section of chaps, blokes, types or whatever. In the main, the majority of these men play a splendid part in the game without ever really leaving an imprint or a name for themselves.

Occasionally though, great players become household names through their exploits at a high level and some administrators etch their names into the history of the game.

We have too, those fellows who have not quite made the top grade on the field - perhaps undeservedly - or have helped to construct the working fabric of the game but in their own way have achieved just as much in their actions to epitomise the fact that rugger is a way of life for true sportsmen of all classes.

Such a man was Brian Strong. It is gathered that his first outings as a player were to make up numbers in a ship's side, playing wherever the boat happened to dock. From such a baptism to the game he ascended to the lower echelons of Richmond where his strength and willingness to learn the art of propping took him way up the club. But it did not stop there, for he went on to appear for Middlesex and for London Counties - not many players have gone so far from a relatively late beginning on the field.

His efforts for whatever side he was in were always of the 100% variety as too were Brian's contributions to touring. This aspect of the fame was probably the area in which those of us who were privileged to be with him on these occasions recall most. After a hard afternoon on the field and lusty comments in the bath, he would really take control of the evening's festivities and the sound "oh what a marff, what a norff and sarff" echoing through the stillness of a bush Kenya evening is never to be forgotten.

By trade Brian was a pipe welder and in rugby circles he carried on his welding - joining all of those who knew him wherever the game took him into a common unit of camaraderie and fellowship. We are privileged to have known and enjoyed his company and we stage this match today in a spirit of happy memory to one of the really great characters to emerge both on and off the field."

During the season the national Press noted ' A rugby seminar held by Richmond to examine links between London junior and senior clubs provided groundwork for future talks rather than immediate dividends. Inevitably, the usual grumbles about poaching of players and unwillingness to grant fixtures were aired. It was more novel to hear the question raised whether there were too many senior clubs in London, and should they be restricted in the number of teams they ran?

London has ten major clubs, including the Irish, Scottish and Welsh exiles. Tradition would never allow mergers with a view to forming stronger combinations. There was a feeling at the meeting, however, that if they were all limited to four sides at the most, there would be a greater leavening of players for junior clubs to absorb. Overall standards at a wider base would be raised.

A properly organised feeder system which should work in both directions between junior and senior clubs was also discussed. Junior clubs have never stood in the way of a player wishing to better himself, but it has tended to be one-way traffic and players should return more frequently to their junior clubs later in their careers to put something back in the game at that level.

An old sore this, and an ideal which, in fact, is achieved more often than is realised. Richmond, the hosts, were able to cite the case of their international centre, T.J.Brooke, who returned to Warlingham with such beneficial results, after winning his caps in the 1960s. How any two-way feeder system could be enforced in an amateur game, it was agreed, would also remain a problem.

More feasible, perhaps for the future, to follow the pattern in Wales by which senior clubs have an arrangement with local junior sides if they wish to borrow a player for a specific Saturday.

Two subjects when probably more heads nodded unanimously in agreement than at any other moment came when aspects of the game in France and New Zealand were discussed. Roger Shackleton, the Richmond captain, who has played in France, said it had left him firmly against the French system of leagues, involving promotion and relegation. Limited competition was all right but, as a staple diet, it had caused play in France to become too rough and rugged. The New Zealand system of intensive coaching and competition for boys from the age of seven onwards was similarly felt to be alien to the spirit of the English game. Although all junior clubs in Middlesex and Surrey were invited, the attendance was poor and, in spite of a second meeting, no firm ground for the future was established.

1978/9

Commander J. Fred Stoy R.N (Ret'd), a long standing member of the club and former Membership Secretary, was voted in as President supported by Alan Skeats as Secretary and Roger Shackleton as Captain. In the role of Treasurer, Terry O'Hanlon, our former scrum-half in the full game and in Sevens, took the reins and the chairmanship of the Executive Committee passed to Tony Vyvyan. The Coaching Panel was headed by Dave Rollitt (of England, Bristol and Richmond fame) supported by Ken Morley, Colin Holman and Nigel Wilson.

The Captain organised a north country trip to start the season, staying in a minus five star hotel in the middle of Preston docks but, in spite of that, Preston Grasshoppers were overcome 28-6 and Vale of Lune 18-9. Then Wasps were our visitors but went away empty handed 6-9 before, in away matches, Richmond fell to Northampton 18-29, Bedford 19-21 and Rosslyn Park 3-24. October brought little joy. London Welsh came to us and won 6-4 before a visit to Welford Road brought no points but 12 to Leicester - then Oxford University travelled and returned with a 15-13 win before a home game gave us the edge over Cambridge University 8-3.

Although November gave a good initial scoreline at home versus Llanelli 23-6, the match was marred by the "Ralston Affair" in which our former Captain was raked on the head by the opposition, severing an artery and causing a wound that required thirty-two stitches. The media coverage was enormous and dragged on for many weeks both in the press and on television and was reported as far away as Australia. Requests to the opposition gave the response that no player had admitted to the offence so that no action could be taken. However, in answer to further questions, the Welsh side suspended all eight of its forwards in the hope that the aggressor would own up. No such admittance was forthcoming and, in spite of protests by Richmond, the Llanelli pack was re-instated. Meetings were sought with the opposition committee who several times suggested venues - always in Wales and resisting our requests for a halfway site. Each time a meeting was agreed Llanelli cancelled it on various pretexts e.g. that evening there was junior match at Stradey Park. The media became increasingly vitriolic about the lack of progress and various Richmond officials were assailed by press and television for not making any advance on discovery of the culprit, as if we had perpetrated the incident, and in spite of Llanelli's prevarication in arranging to meet us.

Some several weeks passed during which some rugby writers suggested "safety boots" because "synthetic materials as much as cynical modern methods are contributing to injuries like Ralston's" (surely a rake is a rake whatever the material and should not be tolerated) and matters remained unresolved.

Eventually, however, two officials of each club met at a rendezvous near Marlborough but our opponents still offered no solution to the problem of finding the perpetrator of the act and, as a consequence, Richmond withdrew from all fixtures with the "Scarlets". Some years later there was talk of a resumption of games between the two sides but Llanelli averred that they had no free Saturdays.

Amidst all the press hiatus Richmond played on, beating Harlequins 28-11 at Twickenham and losing twice to London Scottish (away) 12-19 and in Wales at Swansea 17-30 before snow put a stop to the game at Coventry. Rosslyn Park and Blackheath came to us and went away winners by 9-6 and 13-11 respectively. Harlequins came to The Athletic Ground and lost 16-18 whilst the last game of the year meant our defeat at Wilmslow 7-18.

Weather cancelled the opening fixture of 1979 v Wasps before Saracens travelled and drew 13-13, then a trip to Newcastle resulted in Gosforth winning 9-3. The John Player first round at Kingsholm against Gloucester also suffered weatherwise as did the following game at Headingley but then the Cup was on again and our 9-9 draw gave Richmond a win on the away side principle. A nasty winter as we could not play Bristol away then Gloucester's neighbours Matson came up for the cup and suffered a 3-22 defeat which we followed with a home win over London Scottish 23-8.

Gloucester were played again with the margin being 7-3 to us at home before (again) weather stopped the match at The Reddings against Moseley, whom we did play the following week in the cup only to go down 3-27. We entertained Metropolitan Police and our win was 19-12 but no points were scored in the 0-20 defeat at Neath. The last match of the season resulted in a 35-24 win at Nottingham.

This season's photograph featured the following players: Dave Croydon, Willie Dickinson, Hilary Glean, Gary Greenwood, Michael Hess, Nick Mallett (later Manager of South Africa national XV) Terry O'Hanlon, Nick Preston, Chris Pritchard, Chris Ralston, Ian Ray, Dave Rollitt, Chris Sharpe, Alf Shortland, Rick Taylor, Jim Thorn, Neil Vinter and David Willis. During the year, more honours as Nick Preston was capped for England and W.G.Boyd Morrison III for the USA.

1979/80

The President, Fred Stoy, remained in office as did Terry O'Hanlon (Treasurer) and Tony Vyvyan in charge of the Executive Committee. However, there was a new Secretary in John Castle, a relative newcomer to the club but in his own words "brainy", while the mantle of Captaincy fell on the shoulders of Michael Hess with a coaching panel chaired by Tony Bucknall aided by Ken Morley and Colin Holman. Mainly in the 1st XV were Adrian Barnes, Willie Dickinson, Gary Greenwood, Alan Mort, Michael Oliviera, Rick Pearson, Chris Pritchard, Chris Ralston, Roger Shackleton, Chris Sharpe, Bob Taylor, Jim Thorn, David Whibley, David Willis and Peter Winder.

The home games to start the season showed wins over Wasps 29-19 and Northampton 22-11. Then, five successive losses were suffered - at home versus Bedford 3-36 and Rosslyn Park 9-25, away to London Welsh 17-27, home again to Leicester 13-28 and at Iffley Road against Oxford University 3-9. The match with Leicester was also an Old Players' Reunion when we received unexpected guests in the form of the Prime Minister of Rhodesia, Ian Smith (and some of his entourage), who had broken off talks about the future of his country with our P.M. Harold Wilson to attend this game because of his rapprochement with Richmond during our tour to his country in 1976.

A bounce back - four wins in a row, at Grange Road where Cambridge University were beaten 21-3, at the County Ground, Exeter where the home side lost 9-40 and then a double at home over Harlequins 24-9 and London Scottish 13-10. Two more home games went 50:50 with a 6-35 loss to Swansea and a 9-3 victory against Coventry. In December, travels to Roehampton, Rectory Field and Twickenham showed losses of 6-35 to Rosslyn Park, 12-17 to Blackheath and 10-22 to Harlequins - only redeemed by a home win 16-0 when we played Saracens.

The start of 1980 did not bring a lot of joy as we did not win in January, suffering a 3-7 loss to Wasps away, a 6-6 drew with London Irish at The Avenue, another defeat at home to Gosforth 9-37 and a 6-6 home draw with Gloucester in the John Player Cup but, on the away side rule, we were the losers.

February saw us host Headingley (won 18-9), Blackheath (won 13-3) and Bristol (lost 5-13) before, at Rugby, we came home winners 35-0. March was worse with an away loss to London Scottish 3-15, another defeat away 15-22 v Bedford before two home empty-handed games Moseley 3-8 and Bath 15-27.

After the trauma of the previous season's horrific injury to Chris Ralston, Richmond were pleased to stage a match in his honour and, on the 23rd March, a crowd of 1,500 turned out to pay tribute to Chris Ralston's eighteen years with the club covering five hundred appearances. His standing in the game was underlined by the number of leading players who appeared in his International XV to play Richmond.

Chris captained the side which included Charles Ralston (Rosslyn Park), David Trick (Bath and England), Peter Warfield (Rosslyn Park and England) Rick Gordon (London Scottish), Gordon Wood (London Scottish), Alan Old (Sheffield and England), Steve Smith (Sale and England); Fran Cotton (Sale and England), Ken Kennedy (London Irish and Ireland), Eddie Barlow (Rosslyn Park), Willie John McBride (Ballymena and Ireland), Tony Bucknall (Richmond and England), Tony Neary (Broughton Park and England), Andy Ripley (Rosslyn Park and England) with replacement David Rollitt (Richmond and England). Top referee Norman Sansom took charge of the match, supported by the "young" stalwarts Graham Tardif and Alan Skeats as touch judges.

Against this array of talent our XV performed very creditably to go down by 40-58, the highlights of the game including a try by Chris Ralston himself and three from Peter Winder in a Richmond team that also comprised Mark Pyrgos, Alan Mort, Ian Ray, Colin Lambert; Roger Shackleton, Chris Pritchard, Alf Shortland, Neil Vinter, Brian Hester, Michael Hess (Capt.), Peter Harding, Ray Edwards, Steve Hughes and Gary Greenward with replacements Nick Preston, Graham Gilbert, John Pickin, Robin Robins (who appeared in his twenty first year for Richmond) and Neil Dobson.

The tribute in the programme notes recorded that:
"Undoubtedly one of the most popular figures in rugby is Christopher Wayne

Ralston and today we can appreciate his playing value and service to the game and Richmond in particular.

Chris was born in Hendon and educated at King Williams, Isle of Man. He joined Richmond in the early sixties and worked his way through the club to achieve "Star" status. He first played for Middlesex when in the Vikings and, as we know, last year took the county to win the championship as Captain.

Chris won his first cap in England's centenary game against Scotland in 1971 and played against the President's Overseas XV before leaving his first season in the championship. He toured the Far East with England in 1971 and South Africa in 1972 when the team won at Ellis Park. The greatest achievement was to come - in 1974 he was selected for the British Lions and went with the all-conquering tour of South Africa.

Chris has gathered all the playing honours of the game with which we are all familiar - British Lions, England (twenty-two caps), Barbarians, London Counties, Middlesex and numerous representative XVs. The Richmond Club of which he was Captain in 1974 and 1975 is justifiably proud of his formidable career and greatly appreciates the honours he has accumulated under the old gold, red and black colours. He has now been elected a Vice-President of the club.

Today he joins the eminent stars to play Richmond, which will go some way to mark the success of one of the finest line-out jumpers in the world to the game of rugby union.

Congratulations Chris Ralston and many thanks."

Two more games this season when Metropolitan Police entertained us at Imber Court but lost 3-22 and then at Ireland Avenue, Beeston, Richmond suffered a 6-22 beating.

Chapter Three

The Eighties

1980/81

Fred Stoy, John Castle, Tony Vyvyan and Michael Hess retained their positions in the club but Terry O'Hanlon was succeeded as Treasurer by Bill Carnaby, having given up his tremendous leaps (1 foot) at second row. There were more changes in the Coaching Panel with Colin Holman as Chairman aided by Ken Morley and Pat Lavery, one of the stars of our successful sevens.

This was not a good season as far as results went with only nine wins, one draw and twenty-two losses. This started with three victories - at Molesey Road when we beat Esher 42-12 followed by a home win over Metropolitan Police 23-7 in the new London Merit Table, then a 16-10 defeat away against Wasps in the same table. The end of September gave Northampton a home victory 27-9 a and, following again in the East Midlands, Richmond suffered a 3-19 loss versus Bedford.

A slight recovery when visitors London Welsh went down 10-21 in the Merit Table but the remainder of October produced losses to Leicester 6-38 away, to Oxford University 0-3 and Cambridge University 3-18, both at home. A visit to Camborne brought a 40-4 win but Richmond could only manage a Merit Table 3-3 draw with Harlequins away. Another Merit Table away game gave London Scottish a narrow 6-3 win which was followed by three away defeats at Swansea 0-42, at Roehampton by Rosslyn Park 6-28 (Merit Table) and against Coventry 6-13.

No other wins in 1980 when Rosslyn Park outscored us again 11-3 at home and The Athletic Ground crowd witnessed a Merit Table loss 6-11 to Blackheath and a Harlequins win by 4-0. The home crowd was disappointed again in January, with victors being Wasps 24-6 and London Irish in the Merit Table, 13-10. The Gosforth match away was cancelled before our home tie versus Bath in the John Player Cup resulted in a 6-12 defeat. A little pride was salvaged at Green Road, Southgate in another Merit Table match where Richmond outplayed Saracens 17-0, and at Bridge Road when Headingley gave way to us 3-9, but then very little went right.

Blackheath won 14-13 at home as did Bristol 20-10 at the Memorial Ground, then West Country guests Cheltenham had a 19-3 victory before the

Centenary match against London Scottish produced a 4-7 loss. A trip to Aberavon did not change our luck, the home side out-scoring us 24-4 and, in the Midlands, Moseley enjoyed a 16-3 win. Bath were defeated 25-13 on their ground but a visit to Neath gave the home side a 16-6 win, only redeemed a week later at home by scoring 20 points to Nottingham's 15. Richmond finished 5th in the London Merit Table.

The main players in the 1st XV were Willie Dickinson, David Gavins, Peter Gibson, Steve Hughes, Alan Mort, Mike Oliveira, Rick Pearson, Joe Pickin, Mark Pyrgos, Chris Ralston, Ian Ray, Roger Shackleton, Chris Sharpe, Alf Shortland, Tony Watkinson, David Whibley, Dave Willis and Peter Winder.

1981/2

The Presidency passed to Alan Skeats. Nigel Quinnen, Oxford Blue before joining us and holder of the Varsity Match record in kicking goals, became Secretary. Bill Carnaby carried on as Treasurer and the new Captain was Chris Sharpe with Tony Vyvyan still in control of the Executive. Pat Lavery was in charge of coaching with Ken Morley and Colin Holman still aboard and they were joined by John Hunter (of Borough Road College) and Jim Smallwood (master of Hampton School).

Players involved in a reasonable first half of the season but a poor second half included Barry Crawshaw, Micky Conner, Jim Dyson, Trevor Evans, Steve Faktor, John Fenton, Tony Hamilton, Mike Hess, Martin Humberstone, Simon Jackson, Shaun Kelly, Phil Lusted, Jim McKenzie, Neil (Nelly) Vinter, Robin Osborne, Jeff Probyn, Alf Shortland, Martin Slagter, Jim Thorn, David Whibley, Neil Whitehead and Laurence Williams. Back again to the West Country to open the season and this brought three victories - over Torquay Athletic 20-15, Brixham 12-9 and Bridgwater and Albion 13-10 before an evening match away with Oxford Old Boys resulted in a 32-3 win. Our first Merit Table game at home gave Wasps a 27-6 win and then Northampton came to Richmond and won 25-12. An evening match against Abbey at Emmer Road gave us a 23-6 win followed by a home victory against Bedford 16-6.

The first Merit Table game in October at Old Deer Park gave London Welsh the edge 14-10 before Leicester were held at home to a 6-6 draw. On their home grounds, Richmond disposed of Oxford University 15-3 and Cambridge University 31-0 but the Merit Table was not going too well as we crashed 9-18 to Rosslyn Park at The Athletic Ground.

November's first fixture was an interesting departure from normal club matches. Ballymena, who had previously played against northern England XVs, found that these clubs were refusing to travel to Northern Ireland because of the troubles, so Syd Millar, a great bulwark of Irish rugby and later Lions manager, asked the President if we would consider filling one of their empty Saturdays. The Executive endorsed the proposal and, perhaps because of the excellent hospitality, Ballymena saw us off 13-6. Maybe it was worth it for all the Bushmills the following day!

Back to routine with two Merit Table games - the first gave us a home win over Harlequins 28-6 but, again at home, we failed to score against London Scottish's 28 points. Another new venture was a trip to West Hartlepool resulting in a 13-12 victory, but then December was dismal because Coventry came to us and won 9-0 before the weather interfered with three away matches at Rosslyn Park, Blackheath (Merit Table) and Harlequins, now playing at The Stoop Memorial Ground.

December's Annual Dinner at the Café Royal provided a highlight of the year because of the amusing and pungent speech of Denis Thatcher, a former referee and the husband of the Prime Minister.

On the field, no better in January as home team Wasps won 20-15. The Merit Table game versus London Irish away and a home game with Gosforth were both weather affected and then guests Metropolitan Police beat us 20-10 in the John Player Cup. The only victory was the Merit Table defeat of Saracens 38-10 at The Athletic Ground.

February started with a home win over Headingley but we lost consecutively to visitors Blackheath 3-9, Bristol 7-15 and London Irish 12-15. However we did achieve revenge over London Scottish in March in the away fixture 15-7. The rest of March was as bad as February, suffering three home defeats by Sheffield 10-16, Moseley 6-21 and Bath 9-14 before the Metropolitan Police fixture was cancelled.

Only two more games remained resulting in a 50/50 situation having beaten Neath at home 6-3 but going down to Nottingham at Beeston 6-21.

In the London Merit Table we finished a disappointing eighth. At Easter, there was a 1st XV tour to Guernsey with an opening game giving us a 44-0 win against a Selection XV. The island team were then faced and again victory was ours, by 26-0.

A productive year for players as Tony Kent, Dave Allen, James Espey, Nigel Wilson, David Fangen and David Buchanan fathered girls while Willie Dickinson and Tony Bucknall sired boys.

1982/3

Presidency, Secretaryship, Treasurer and Captain remained in the same hands but Nigel Quinnen took control of the Executive. Pat Lavery claimed the Coaching Panel with other helpers being John Hunter and Chris Ralston.

Shades of last season as only seven games were won before the New Year and only two (with one draw) after that. September was the best month as victories were recorded at Torquay 27-10 and Paignton 35-0 before the Merit Table match at Sudbury gave Wasps an 18-11 win. We then had victories away over Northampton 20-9 and Bedford 28-6 but, in the John Player Cup at home, Metropolitan Police were the victors 7-3. The second Merit Table game produced an away win for London Welsh 12-3 then we suffered at Leicester losing 8-21. An evening game when we were hosts to London New Zealand produced a 36-12 win and this was followed at home by victory 19-8 against Oxford University. Then followed a sequence of seven losses - at home to Cambridge University 0-25, at Roehampton where Rosslyn Park outplayed us 19-0 before we entertained (without the Bushmills) Ballymena and they returned home 31-12 victors. Two away Merit Table games gave wins to Harlequins 28-12 and London Scottish 23-7 and the losing run went on at St Helens when Swansea won 31-6 during which a most regrettable incident occurred.

A line-out had been formed but, before the ball was thrown in, Barry Crawshaw was felled by a "haymaker" that broke his jaw.

The offence was seen by all in the main stand except the members of the Swansea committee who afterwards could not understand how the injury had happened. Unfortunately, the referee had not seen the vicious incident and was unable to comment, even though Richmond were conclusive in citing the individual responsible.

The Crawshaw family considered legal action but eventually, in consultation with the Richmond committee, they agreed to let the matter rest; the Swansea committee was unresponsive and nothing was resolved, in spite of much backing from the media.

At Coundon Road, Coventry won 23-4 before Rosslyn Park were entertained and, at last, a victory by 16-9 but Blackheath came to us for a Merit Table game and went away 9-4 winners before weather caused the cancellation of the Harlequins fixture. The New Year started with a victory at home over Wasps 16-3 only for Richmond to fail again at home 6-16 in a Merit Table clash with London Irish and then go on to lose 6-18 at Gosforth and 6-13 at Blundell Sands versus Waterloo in the John Player Cup. The month ended with a 10-10 draw at Saracens in the Merit Table.

A visit to Headingley gave the home side an advantage 20-10 before icy conditions prevented away games at Blackheath and Bristol taking place. The next venue was Llynfi Road, Maesteg where the home XV won 28-9 but weather intervened again and our home match with London Scottish was called off before visitors Gloucester went down 7-24. A week later Moseley were visited and we lost 3-6 and a trip to Bath gave the home XV a 32-18 triumph. Nottingham were entertained but the losing streak continued and we went down 12-22, before we ended with a home game versus Metropolitan Police, the result being a 22-13 victory.

An Easter tour was undertaken to the Netherlands but the only record for this tournament occasion showed that Richmond won convincingly versus R.C. t'Gool, Nijmegen and a President's XV but lost 0-9 to Manchester side, Davenport.

It was with regret that the club recorded the sad death, in his early sixties, of John Black, who had given such long and exemplary service as Treasurer.

During the season Chris Sharpe utilised the services of the following players: Keith Bassom, Colin Green, Tony Hamilton, Chris Heather, Peter Hearn, Mike Hess, Sean Kelly, Pat Lavery, Simon Pennock, Nick Preston, Jeff Probyn, Martin Slagter, Jerry Smith, Jim Thorn, Neil Vinter, Ian Warren, David Whibley, Neil Whitehead, Laurence Williams and Phil (Tonka) Williams.

Our lowest place yet in the London Merit Table as we were ninth.

1983/4

Alan Skeats (President) and Nigel Quinnen (Secretary) carried on but there was a new Treasurer in Geoffrey Clarke, Richmond's penetrative centre of yesteryear. There was also a new Captain in Martin Slagter and Mike Humphreys, a product of Cheltenham who brought height and expertise to our second row, assumed control of the Executive. The Coaching Panel changed yet again, still led by Pat Lavery but including Chris Ralston, Dave Rollitt and an everlasting back, Tony Sharp.

The Captain enjoyed a slightly better season then those of the preceding years and filled his XV with the players as nominated on the team photograph: Kevin Bassom, Bill Biddell, Mike Catt, Micky Conner, Richard Crawford, Ray Edwards, Steve Faktor, John Fenton, Dave Guyatt, Andy Hampel, Michael Hess, Martin Humberstone, Andy (Boomer) Jones, Sean Kelly, Chris Mackaness, Andy Maren, Andy Peck, Simon Pennock, Nick Preston, Jeff Probyn, Bruce Roxburgh, Martin Slagter, Hugh Stevenson, Jim Thorn, Neil Whitehead and Phil Williams.

The club had to play a qualifying round for the John Player Cup to start the season and this at home gave us a 42-3 win over Civil Service. But back to earth at The Athletic Ground when Wasps (Merit Table Game) took away the spoils 40-7, followed by a loss to Northampton 13-20.

The first round of the Cup produced a 22-16 victory over Saracens at home but Bedford came to us and won 19-3 followed by another Merit Table loss away at London Welsh by 6-16. Leicester were our next visitors and they went away victors 10-0, after which we travelled to the universities winning 24-3 at Oxford but managing only a 26-26 draw at Cambridge.

At last a Merit Table win when, at home, Richmond outscored Rosslyn Park 22-15 but an away trip to Sheffield proved unsuccessful as we lost 21-25. Two home Merit Table games gave us points as we beat Harlequins 17-12 and London Scottish 9-7 before visitors Swansea returned home with a 43-8 win. The next cup round gave us a home tie with US Portsmouth which we won convincingly 43-0. Rosslyn Park away produced another Richmond win 20-15, followed by victory at Blackheath 28-9 in another Merit Table game. On Christmas Eve at The Stoop no festive cheer for us as Harlequins won 14-11 and the year ended with our 21-12 win against Saracens at home.

January was a duff month with three losses; Wasps away 14-33, Merit Table away versus London Irish 3-22 and against visitors Gosforth 3-15, before inclement weather produced no game at Waterloo.

Nuneaton were our hosts in the John Player Cup where we achieved a 9-6 win and then Blackheath came to us and lost 12-29. Another sequence of defeats gave best to Bristol at The Athletic Ground 21-25 and Waterloo at home in the cup 19-26, before London Scottish in a home fixture saw us off 29-10. Gloucester were next to inflict defeat on Richmond at Kingsholm, the score being 28-14 in the host's favour.

Moseley travelled down and were beaten 13-9 a week before Richmond's visit to Rodney Parade, Newport gave the home side a massive 51-6 victory. The last Merit Table game at Imber Court produced 10 points to Metropolitan Police's 3 and that was followed by a home defeat of Neath 18-17 whilst the last match at Nottingham resulted in a 19-7 win for the home side. The final listing in the London Merit Table placed Richmond at sixth.

Kudos off the pitch for club member Nick Oatway in Harlesden when he drove his car at an armed raider who landed on his bonnet and hit a second raider. Twelve thousand pounds was recovered then Nick continued the chase in his car until the culprit hit a lamppost and escaped.

The case eventually went to the Old Bailey where there were praises for his extraordinary bravery.

1984/5

For the first time in many years all the leading officials continued in their positions although yet again Pat Lavery's Coaching Panel saw changes the others involved being Dave Rollitt (1st XV) Tony Sharp, Nigel Wilson and Derek Wyatt (ex England, Bedford and Richmond and later to become M.P for Sittingbourne and Sheppey). A notable newcomer to the club was Takeo (Tiger) Shizuka who had captained Japan and won 22 caps. Regrettably, the up and down pattern of the preceding years was not to change.

Richmond were, as others, embroiled now in two Merit Tables. The opening match saw a visit from West Hartlepool resulting in our 21-15 win but the first Merit Table game at Wasps gave the hosts a 12-7 win.

In the East Midlands, Northampton gave way to us 0-9 and then Bedford suffered 6-19. However Merit Table games seemed not to be Richmond's forte as both Rosslyn Park at home won 16-15 and then London Welsh came to us and went home winners 35-16. Humiliation followed at Leicester where the 'Tigers' out-pointed us massively 55-21, but recovering a home win over Oxford University 14-3 was small comfort for the following week's loss - also at home - to Cambridge University 4-24.

November commenced with what was believed to be, at that point in time, Richmond's biggest ever win, when Exeter crept back to Devon having conceded 76 points without replying. Then, as ever, back to a string of losses with four away defeats - against Harlequins 4-29, London Scottish 9-14 (Merit Table), Swansea 14-34 and Coventry 0-37 and a home loss to Rosslyn Park 13-37.

The end of December meant three Merit Table fixtures, the first two at home and the last away and all became wins - over Blackheath 24-23, Harlequins 13-6 and Saracens 36-31.

Two opening games in January at home to Wasps and London Irish (Merit Table) were weather affected and three losses ensued at Gosforth 6-16, 0-29 against Gloucester in the cup 3rd Round away and at Headingley 7-38. The Army were entertained and beaten 14-6 before the Bristol game was lost to weather and a 16-23 loss suffered at London Irish.

March opened with two home wins when we scored 15 points to London Scottish's 13 and 61 to Northern's 13 before we journeyed to take on Moseley at The Reddings, the outcome being disaster at 15-35. Ebbw Vale came up to visit us and were beaten 20-10 and, finally, Metropolitan Police in a Merit Table game were also visitors with the result being 16-15 to them, before Northampton travelled to The Athletic Ground and carried the spoils 17-9. The aforementioned Japanese connection was strengthened in April when we entertained Gakushi Rugger Club but, sadly, no result is to hand. No joy in the London Merit Table as we ended a lowly ninth.

The season's prominent players were Bill Biddell, Micky Conner, Richard Crawford, Willie Dickinson, Ricky Forde, Dave Guyatt, Andy Hampel, John Heaton, Michael Hess, Martin Humberstone, Sean Kelly, Andy Maren, Chris Mills, Simon Pennock, Nick Preston, Jeff Probyn, Bruce Roxburgh, Martin Slagter, Jerry Smith, Simon Smith and Jim Thorn.

1985/6

Although the positions of the President, Secretary, Treasurer and Captain remained as before, the fixture book, strangely, did not record the Chairmanship of the Executive - only the names of the members. The Coaching Panel was reduced to two members viz. David Rollitt (1st XV) and Derek Wyatt.

In a season that gave the same sort of pattern of wins and losses as in earlier years Martin Slagter relied largely on the players listed here; Simon Attfield, Steve Allum, Richard Castleton (who was tragically killed in a road accident), Micky Conner, Peter Combe, Doug Cooper, Geoff Crawford, John Cullen, Martin Drane, Ray Edwards, Rickey Forde, Dave Gavins, Dougie Goodwin, Dave Guyatt, Andy Hampel, John Heaton, Seijo Hirao, Martin Humberstone, Andy Janes, Chris MacDonald, Tim Martineau, Chris Mills, Simon Pennock, Nick Preston, Bruce Roxburgh, David Sole and Simon Smith.

The club was involved in the London One Merit Table, as in past seasons, and now also in the John Smith Merit Table encompassing clubs up and down the country. In the following notes they are denoted as LM (London Merit) and JS (John Smith) whilst the cup remained in the sponsorship of John Player.

The whole of the month of September was concerned with one or other of the above competitions and commenced with two losses versus Saracens 3-13 (LM and JS) at home, then Waterloo 7-55 (JS) away, before a qualifying cup draw brought Old Gaytonians to The Athletic Ground for a qualifying round and we progressed 40-9. Wasps were the next visitors and were the victors 13-7 (LM) preceding another cup qualifying round when we hosted Metropolitan Police and won 52-20. Northampton faced us at Franklin's Gardens and scored 19 to our 7 (JS) before, in the 1st round of the cup, our home fixture with London Irish brought a 21-14 victory. October marked the debut of Seijo Hirao, another Japanese international and a cult figure in his own land.

Bedford here were next to go down to us 15-19 (JS) and, at London Welsh,

Richmond got two Merit Table wins by 18-12 (LM and JS) before Leicester came to us and won 27-13. A match at Iffley Road gave Richmond a 46-32 advantage over Oxford University then, drawn at home again in the cup, Cheshunt our visitors lost 6-30.

South Wales Police were visited but we returned empty-handed to a score of 12-18 and the next two home games were Harlequins (LM) in which we lost 7-11 and London Scottish (LM) when the score was 25-17 against us. Swansea were faced at home as were Orrell (JS) but both went against Richmond by 9-27 and 9-12 respectively.

December brought Coventry down (JS) and they lost 11-20 which we followed by beating Rosslyn Park (LM and JS) 29-12 but, at Blackheath (also LM and JS), the home side notched up 11 points to our nil. The last game of the year versus Metropolitan Police (LM) was postponed for a week (weather) but, when played, it was a narrow 25-24 win for Richmond.

London Irish at Sunbury (LM and JS) ran out winners 24-16 before three home games resulted in defeats against Gosforth 4-6, Blackheath in the John Player 3rd round 7-12 and against visitors Headingley 0-8. The winter caught up with us and cancellations resulted in no matches with Maesteg (away), Bristol and London Irish (both home) and London Scottish (away).

On resumption of the season, Richmond won 19-13 at Rosslyn Park but went down at home to Moseley 17-22 and Bath 13-30 away before drawing 9-9 against Neath at home. The season finished at Nottingham in the most dismal fashion with a 10-30 defeat.

In the London Merit Table our position was halfway whilst in Table B of the John Smith competition we ended tenth.

Regrettably, the deaths occurred during the season of Past President Frank Mennim and our former captain Colin Allan.

1986/7

Changes at the top of the club saw Robin Robins, our former back row player (whose father had also played for the club and gave his life for his country in the Second World War) installed as President and Andy Hampel as Captain. Nigel Quinnen carried on as Secretary, Geoffrey Clarke as Treasurer and Mike Humphreys as Executive Chairman. Derek Wyatt chaired coaching helped by Pat Lavery, Michael Hess (who kept goal for Wesminster School before he saw the light and joined Richmond), Willie Dickinson (our prop unlucky never to have been capped by England) and Brian Hester (another prop who had captained Hertfordshire).

This season the London Merit Table had been dropped and, apart from the

John Player Cup, all attention was focused on the John Smith Merit Table referred to hereafter, as last season, as (JS).

Opening home games gave a 51-9 win over Streatham-Croydon but the first JS match showed a loss to Waterloo 14-33. Wasps were met away when the home XV registered a 25-15 success. A week later at home Northampton outplayed Richmond 49-9 (JS) but, to balance things out, Bedford were beaten at Goldington Road 15-9 (JS) and at home we scored 30 points to London Welsh 14 (JS).

The Welford Road crowd saw Leicester outplay us 36-19, but then came five wins over Oxford University (home) 11-9, Cambridge University (home) 42-12, Gosforth (away) 21-12 (JS) Liverpool St Helens (away) 19-10 (JS) and London Scottish (away) 23-21.

However, the momentum was lost and, in the first of three travels, Swansea won 15-12 in a game marred by another regrettable incident when, allegedly, a relative of the 'All Whites' player in the 'Crawshaw affair' inflicted a severe eye injury on Chris Mills. Another home player was sent off at the time but the perpetrator remained on the pitch and, in spite of representations, Swansea Club officials refused to acknowledge that the wrong player had suffered an 'early bath' and, unfortunately, the matter was left unresolved. Away Orrell beat us 23-0 and Coventry out-pointed Richmond 23-12. The year finished with three home fixtures, the results being wins over Rosslyn Park 12-10 (JS), Blackheath 28-6 (JS), but a loss 10-11 to Harlequins.

South Wales Police were with us in January and lost 10-30 before London Irish travelled and went away 7-14 losers (JS) before facing us again in the cup when again Richmond won (away) by 9-5. The next two Merit Table matches were scheduled versus Saracens away (cancelled) and at Headingley where we lost 3-19, similar to the following week when Bristol ran in winners here by 18-3 in the Cup 4th round.

Bristol were also faced next as a normal fixture and again they won (at home), by an 18-12 margin, and then a journey to Maesteg brought a 15-54 defeat. London Scottish were met at home with a 20-9 Richmond win but, in entertaining Gloucester and Exeter University, we had mixed fortunes losing the first game 6-23 but winning the second 26-22. Moseley and Newport away gave us no joy, both being reverses with scores of 3-32 and 8-59. The following day we hosted Club Universitaire de Rugby Association (Curda) from Paraguay and just pipped them 19-18. Metropolitan Police left Imber Court and lost 6-10 whilst, at The Gnoll, Neath triumphed 42-25 and here at home Nottingham scored a runaway victory 57-0. Creditable efforts in the John Smith Table B as we were runners-up.

The season's main players were Steve Allum, Simon Attfield, Bill Biddell, Steve Brinkley, Pete Combe, Micky Conner, Dougie Cooper, Martin Corr, John Cullen, Martin Drane, Dougie Goodwin, Andy Hampel, John Heaton, Richard Holman, Mark James, Dave Kenningham, Andy Maren, Tim Martineau, Chris Mills, Simon Pennock, Martin Slagter, Simon Smith, David Sole, Jim Thorn, Phil Williams and Charlie Vyvyan.

Another notable feature of the season was the abandonment of a fixture with the Hedgehogs of Cape Town because our coach Derek Wyatt objected to playing any XV associated with apartheid. Wyatt was also the first coach to use a psychologist - but many players were not impressed by this theorism.

1987/8

Robin Robins started his second year as President, but the departure of Nigel Quinnen brought back Alan Skeats as Secretary, supported by Treasurer, Geoffrey Clarke, Executive Chairman, Mike Humphreys, and new Captain, John Cullen. Yet another turnabout for the Coaching Panel as now there were six on it, namely Pat Lavery, Michael Hess, John Fenton, our former back row "wizard", Willie Dickinson, Ray Edwards (our Antipodean forward from Canberra) and Kevan (Dinger) Bell, our ex- forward and wild man from Cornwall. Derek Wyatt remained as 1st XV coach.

The John Smith Merit Table had now gone from the scene and had been replaced by the Courage Clubs Championship, which also covered clubs throughout England. Based on previous results, Richmond were placed in League Two.

The first visitors were Streatham-Croydon who lost 6-26; the first trip away was to suffer a 25-32 loss at Waterloo and the second visitors Wasps went away winners 4-0. Northampton were visited in the Courage Club Championship and we came out on top 16-3 and, away in Ireland at Castle Road, the home club Clontarf went down 10-21 to us before the next Courage game away gave us victory over London Welsh 26-22.

Then, like earlier seasons, we slumped - losing 6-20 at home to Leicester, suffering a 16-12 loss away to Oxford University, losing 8-17 at Sale, being beaten 17-28 at Grange Road against Cambridge University, giving way at Orrell 3-12 before two more losses when Gosforth came to us and won 12-10 and Liverpool St Helens came south and won 13-8 - the last two games being Courage League matches.

London Scottish travelled to us in a Courage game and lost 6-9 whilst, at Beacon Park, Richmond drew with home side Plymouth Albion 9-9. Coventry again came south and were triumphant 22-9, and two Courage matches away saw Richmond go under to Rosslyn Park 12-20 but struggle to a 4-3 win at Blackheath and, finally, Harlequins 46 Richmond 20 was the sad result at The Stoop three days after Christmas.

A visit to Bridgend produced no joy because South Wales Police won 28-4 and this was followed by a Courage defeat against London Irish at Sunbury - the score being 15-17. Rugby came to us and lost 7-9 before we beat Liverpool St Helens 10-6 at home in the third round of the John Player Cup. The Courage game at home versus Saracens was cancelled but, a week later at home, another Courage game resulted in a 14-13 win against Headingley.

The 4th round of the cup matched us against Bristol but at the Memorial Ground we went down 0-34 with another loss a week later - a normal fixture against Bristol at home when they produced another victory, this time by 24-13. Newbridge came to Richmond and lost 14-27 and then London Scottish playing away failed to score against Richmond's 20 points. A visit to Gloucester gave the home side an easy victory 44-12 before, at home, Exeter University beat us 13-10. No match the following week here against Moseley but, the day after, touring side Bulldogs were held to a 12-12 draw.

Final matches against Bedford (home), Metropolitan Police (away), Nottingham (away), and Bedford (home) produced scores of 28-25; regrettably unrecorded; 16-44 and then a cancellation. For the record, Richmond finished in half way position, with League Two showing us in 6th Place.

The season's photograph showed these players Simon Attfield, Dave Basley, Martin Breddy, Peter Combe, Doug Cooper, Paul Crerar, John Cullen, Ricky Forde, David Gavins, Dougie Goodwin, Andy Hampel, "Harry" Harrison, John Heaton, Alf Hellawell, Dave Kenningham, Chris McDonald, Stuart Maxwell, Chris Mills, Simon Pennock, Nick Preston, Derek Rimmer, Mark Roper, Rob Ryden, Paul Seccombe, Martin Slagter, Simon Smith, David Sole, Jim Thorn, Peter Winduss and Victor Ubogu.

1988/9

President Robin Robins was re-installed, as were Geoffrey Clarke as Treasurer and John Cullen as Captain, but the Secretaryship passed to Keith Cresswell (ex Mini-rugby Secretary), Fred Stoy took over as Executive committee Chairman. Like Topsy, the Coaching Panel grew again led by Stefan Czerpak (former Newbury coach) with Derek Wyatt (1st XV coach) leading Micky Conner of scrum half fame, Willie Dickinson, Ray Edwards, Michael Hess, Pat Lavery, Mel Jones (former Norman's secretary) and old second row, Martin Slagter.

The first fixture concerned a visit from Waterloo who had a 17-16 win and, at Heywood Road in a Courage Match, Sale thrashed Richmond 50-9 but, in welcoming Clontarf, Richmond shaded the match 16-15 and then took more Courage points in beating London Welsh 14-3 at home. The difference was 19-3 in Richmond's favour when Pontypridd came to The Athletic Ground but, going to Gosforth (Courage match) we went down 4-16, following which losses were suffered twice at home - against Oxford University 12-16 and, in a Courage game, 12-32 to London Scottish.

At Edgehall Road, Orrell were beaten 23-10 and then, in November in the Cup, (now retitled Pilkington), Richmond went to Finchley at Summers Road where the home side succumbed 6-40. Mixed results in the next three Courage games with an away loss at Blackheath 3-31, but two home wins over Northampton 15-12 and Coventry 12-3. Nottingham were faced at Ireland Avenue where we suffered a 3-27 loss then Metropolitan Police came to Richmond and lost 14-34 and the year ended with two losses - at The Athletic Ground against Leicester 7-16 and Harlequins 7-21.

In January, Rosslyn Park were overcome 26-9 and South Wales Police 25-19, both at home, before, in the Courage Club's Championship, Bedford registered a home win against us 15-3. Wasps at home outscored Richmond 41-16 and a 4th round home cup-tie with Northampton gave us a 6-0 win, then there was a 10-29 defeat at Moseley and exit from the cup at Nottingham, the home side winning 12-9.

Weather cancelled matches at Bristol and Maesteg but, in a home fixture, London Scottish were beaten 16-6 a week before the Courage match with Saracens at home, which was a failure, the score against Richmond being 27-10. In an absolute downpour at Moss Lane, Liverpool St Helens shared a 0-0 draw but the following week's game at Bath was cancelled. Neath at Neath piled up 50 points to our 4, a home game with London Irish (Courage) ended in a 18-18 draw, at Newbridge Richmond lost out 15-25 and the final Courage match at Clarence Field, the opponents being Headingley, produced a result of 12-9 to the home side. This season we dropped to ninth in National League Two.

At John Cullen's elbow were Steve Allum, Clive Baker, Martin Breddy, Mike Catt, Peter Catt, Ewan Clark, Chris Combe, Peter Combe, Keith Cook, Doug Cooper, John Cullen, Paul Farmer, Ricky Forde, Paul Hackett, "Harry" Harrison, Andy Hampel, Nigel Johnson, Dave Kenningham, Martin (Sausage) Livesey, Andy Maren, Chris Morrish, "Mod" Oliviera, John Risman, Rob Ryden, Eddie Saunders, Paul Seccombe, David Sole, Paul Southern and Charlie Vyvyan.

1989/90

The club elected Graham Tardif, the former Westcombe Park, Blackheath and Richmond prop, as President, re-elected Keith Cresswell as Secretary and, in a non-chauvinistic attitude, appointed Mary Forsyth, the player mainly responsible for bringing the Women's XV to Richmond, as Treasurer. The Executive Committee became known as the Management Committee under the chairmanship of Robert Rakison, the former Chairman of the Youth Committee and redoubtable oarsman. On the playing side, the new Captain was Doug Cooper with Stefan Czerpak in charge of coaching with old hands, Willie Dickinson, Michael Hess and Pat Lavery, now joined by our old centre, Ian Ray, and Rob Cunningham (ex Gosforth, Bath and London Scottish).

At last, a season in which wins exceeded losses and progress was made to the quarter final of the Cup. The players mainly responsible for better success were Simon Attfield, Clive Baker, John Bower, Mike Catt, Doug Cooper, Rob Cunningham, Adam Ellery, Andrew Evans, Jim Fallon, John Fenton, Ricky Forde, John Fowler, Dougie Goodwin, Paul Guttridge, Paul Hackett, Alf Hellewell, Glen Jasprizza, Howard Lamb, Martin Livesey, Andy Maren, Paul Morris, Peter Radford, John Risman, Harry Roberts, Rob Ryden, Eddie Saunders, David Sole, Charlie Vyvyan, Simon Waghorn, Rob Whyley and Matt Yeldham.

An away game at Southgate gave Richmond victory over Saracens, and then, at home in the renamed Courage League, Sale were beaten 16-7 before an 18-18 draw at Rosslyn Park and a Courage win at Webb Ellis Road when Rugby went down 16-28. This was a game marred by an injury to hooker Peter Combe, who nearly swallowed his tongue after an "incident". Peter never played again and, regrettably, the matter was unresolved between the two clubs. Orrell came to Richmond and won 20-13 and we travelled to Pontypridd only to concede 22 points to our 13. The Courage League brought Gosforth down to us and we gained a 36-3 win, then away to Metropolitan Police who were eclipsed 12-10 but in Oxford the university recorded a 24-21 win. To the West Country in the Courage League and Plymouth Albion were defeated 12-11 before journeying that way again to meet Barnstaple in the Cup where Richmond won 22-7.

Blackheath came to Richmond for a Courage League game, the scores being even at 15-15 before three away losses to Cambridge University (14-28) and, in the Courage tournament, to Northampton (6-12) and Coventry (18-21). The Combined Services were taken on at Aldershot with our win by 15-8 before we recorded a victory at home against Nottingham 15-11. The last three matches of the year were not in Richmond's favour when, all away, the winners were Bath

16-10, Leicester 44-12 and Harlequins 20-18.

January to April 1990 was the best period for many years with only two losses. Two wins started the year, both at home - over London Welsh 13-0 and South Wales Police 24-16, but then Liverpool St Helens were our visitors and managed 17 points to Richmond's 6 in a Courage League Match. Sheffield came down and lost 14-24 preceding a 3rd round Cup success at Bedford with a score of 12-7, before a cancelled match with Moseley at home. A home tie in the 4th round of the cup was tight with a Richmond 14 Sale 12 result, before next visitors Bristol held us to a 21-21 draw and February ended with the cup Quarter Final when we crashed to Bath 3-35 at home.

A cold start to March saw the game with London Scottish cancelled but five wins followed - at Waterloo 23-13 (Courage League), at home versus Wasps 46-3 and Glamorgan Wanderers 59-21, after which we outscored London Irish in a Courage match at Sunbury 36-12 and Gloucester away 12-10.

The home game with Bedford was cancelled and the season ended with a home win over Newbridge 23-2 and, at The Athletic Ground, Headingley crashed to a tremendous Courage League defeat to the tune of 8-86. Our best season yet in National League Two as we finished third. The season was marred by the sudden death of John Riley, President from 1975 - 1978 and a grand servant of the club on many committees.

Chapter Four

The Nineties

1990/1

Graham Tardif retained the Presidency as did Keith Cresswell (Secretary), Mary Forsyth (Treasurer) and Robert Rakison (Executive Chairman) whilst Mark Hancock was elected as Captain. During the season the Secretary resigned and Alan Skeats took over the reins again. Stefan Czerpak had departed and Rob Cunningham oversaw coaching aided by Michael Hess, Micky Conner and Vinny Codrington, our fly half of considerable promise before he took years out in Canada and currently Secretary of Middlesex C.C.C., also Tim Herman, who had advanced through our junior XVs and coaches Surrey U17s and Dave Hilliard, the ex Basingstoke coach.

The second-half high-note of the previous season was regrettably not maintained with only 10 wins being achieved, offset by two draws and 21 losses. One of the draws was in the opening game at home with the scoreline against Saracens being 23-23 after which the game with intended visitors Basingstoke was cancelled. A visit to Rodney Parade gave Newport the edge 8-6 and, in north London, the Wasps hammered home a 56-3 victory before a visit to Newbridge produced a 19-12 win in our favour. Back home Moseley beat us 23-3 and away trips to Edge Hall Road, Orrell and Beacon Park, Plymouth gave Richmond no joy, the games being lost by scores of 10-12 and 13-19 respectively, the latter game being in the Courage League.

Another three league games resulted in a win at home over Bedford 28-17, a loss away to Rugby 9-28 and a victory over visitors Sale 10-9. Sudbury came to Richmond for the Pilkington Cup but lost 9-26 preceding two league losses against Waterloo (away) 9-25 and London Scottish (home) 15-40. The 3rd Round of the cup meant Liverpool St Helens travelling south and losing 12-13.

At Ireland Avenue in December, Nottingham won the day 29-8 before a cancellation of the Bath fixture at home and a visit to Rosslyn Park where the home XV ran out at 21-9 winners. Harlequins came to us three days before Christmas and lost 20-21 but an end of the year fixture in Bristol meant another failure for Richmond, losing 3-19.

New Year's Day was good, Richmond outscored London Welsh at Old Deer Park 23-16 but, four days later, weather caused the cancellation of the match with Neath at home. At the Rectory Field Blackheath were 12-9 winners but, up at Abbeydale Park, Sheffield were out-pointed 32-10. The following week ended our progress in the Cup, Nottingham winning 24-6 at home. The seaside air at Blackpool Road, Fylde did not do Richmond any good as we came away losers 9-18.

A cold spell caused the calling off of the next two matches - both at home with Coventry (a league game) and Heriot's FP, before a run of four losses involving Gloucester away 8-18, Leicester at home 18-40, a league clash away with Gosforth 3-38 and Glamorgan Wanderers in Cardiff 6-17.

Two home fixtures brought Headingley, who lost 6-17, and Lewes, who lost 6-70, to The Athletic Ground but the game with Boroughmuir in Edinburgh was cancelled. The re-arranged league fixture with Coventry at home meant a 0-13 loss and, at College Grove in another Courage League match, Wakefield won 20-3. Metropolitan Police were met at Imber Court - result another loss for us 6-19 and, in the last home game, we secured a Courage League draw with London Irish 18-18.

The final National League Two table showed disaster as we went down a league having ended in 12th position.

Leading players of the season under Mark Hancock were Jim Ashworth, Jonathan Clarke, Andy Cuthbert, Douggie Elliott, Andrew Evans, Mark Evans, John Fenn, Ricky Forde, James Foster, John Fowler, Dougie Goodwin, Tim Griffin, Paul Guttridge, Nick Hawkins, Mike Hutton, Ian Jackson, Glen Jasprizza, Ian Keary, Howard Lamb, Jonathan Lewis, Martin Livesey, Adrian McKay, Damian Morris, Darryl Patterson, Martin Radford, Rob Ryden, Eddie Saunders, David Sole, Mike Tanner, Sean Williams, Jonathan Willis and Matt Yeldham.

1991/2

The President entered his third term and Mary Forsyth remained in office. Peter Quinnen, the assiduous worker in the youth set-up, was elected as Secretary with Tony Hallett, a noted Heavy and one of the Royal Navy's representatives on the R.F.U, assuming the Chairmanship alongside a new office, that of Director of Rugby - a post filled by Vinny Codrington - overseeing coaches Dave Hilliard, Adrian Alexander (ex Quins and Rugby League) Tim Herman and Chris Humphreys from Bath (for fitness). A former All Black, Kevin Boroevich, took on the duties of Captain and he was to lead his players, namely Richard Banks, Tim Benson, Matt Brown, Doug Cooper, William Deeley, Doug Elliott, James Foster, Dougie Goodwin, Jason Hoad, Mark Hudson, Mike Hutton, Howard Lamb, Jonathan Lewis, Martin Livesey, Chris Lloyd, Adrian McKay, Simon Miller, Rob Ryden, John Satterley, David

Sole, Phil Williams, and Jonathan Willis, to an improved list of results although the first two away matches were defeats by Northampton 16-21 and Saracens 12-34.

Newport came to Richmond and lost 24-28 the week before a Pilkington Cup 1st round draw took the club to Barnstaple where we registered a 26-6 win and then away London Scottish fell to us 14-15. Another win followed at home over Rosslyn Park 9-8 but, at the Recreation Ground, the home side Bath pipped Richmond by the odd point 10-9. Wasps were also the victors at The Athletic Ground 18-13 but the away fixture at Neath was cancelled.

November's fixtures started with Oxford University visiting us and winning 21-9 before the next round of the Cup meant a home win over Blackheath 22-12. At Cross Green, Richmond started the Courage fixtures but went down to Otley 9-19 only to recover at home (league again) against Broughton Park, the score being 20-18. The cup run was over when, at Bramley Road, Saracens put together a 33-9 win before a visit to the Recreation Ground in Redruth - another Courage game - gave Richmond a 9-6 winning margin - in spite of Hell Fire Corner. The league game with Headingley at home fell foul of the weather before fellow Courage League side Askeans were beaten 17-6 at Broad Walk.

1992 was most successful - with eleven wins, one draw and only three losses. A draw started the year - at home to Exeter in the league 16-16, followed by another league win at Fylde 13-12. The London Irish game away was cancelled but Fylde came to us for a friendly and suffered another loss 15-21. In Yorkshire, the Morley XV scored 15 points to Richmond's 12 and another loss followed at home when Nottingham ran out winners 25-12.

Richmond then had the pleasure of hosting Club Atletico Lomas from Buenos Aires, winning 31-16 before entertaining Clifton (league match) and getting a narrow 16-15 victory. Disaster at Welford Road where Leicester ran in 50 points to our 19 but, from then until the end of the season, all the results were victories. In three league games Lydney (at Regentholme) were beaten 18-7, Headingley (at home) 28-13 and Nuneaton (home) 43-6. South Wales Police visited us and lost by an odd point 28-27 after which a league victory was gained at Chandos Park over Roundhay, 50 points to 3. The season finished with two home matches and wins over Metropolitan Police 13-12 and Sheffield in the league 57-3. Bounce back time because winning National League Table 3 meant a return to League 2.

In January, there happened the most unfortunate accident to the youngster Gareth Savin who broke his neck whilst playing for the Under 19s and became tetraplegic. The club set up a Trust to support his permanent need for assistance and contributions have enabled him to live in a specially-adapted residence and he has the use of a car. He remains his cheerful self and is a regular visitor to the ground. Regular charity walks and fund raising continue to ensure 'our promise' to Gareth that he is a member of the Richmond family life.

Regrettably, we recorded the death at ninety-seven years of age of Arthur Cormack, our Treasurer for over forty years and President from 1957 to 1961.

1992/3

A new President in former Captain Steve James who had Tony Hallett as Chairman and Peter Quinnen as Secretary with a new Treasurer, Alistair Law, an accountant and another of our locks with aspirations to greatness. Vinny Codrington remained Director of Rugby and Kevin Boroevich as Captain. Helping the Director of Rugby with coaching were Dave Hilliard (former Senior Team Manager), Roger Uttley (of England, Gosforth and Wasps fame), Tim Herman, Peter Halsall (ex St Benedicts), Dave Rollitt, John Kingston (a Geordie who had played for Cambridge University and Rosslyn Park before successfully (very) training our Under 19 XV), Don Taylor (ex Met Police and oldest-ever Cambridge Blue at 38) with fitness under Chris Humpage.

An early season run-out with Ealing was cancelled before three victories were achieved - the losers being London Welsh (who visited us) 8-21 and Northampton 14-20 (away) and, on the Down Grange ground, Basingstoke 17-32 (where your author ran the line for the last time) Four Courage games followed with mixed results, Nottingham winning at Ireland Avenue 17-12, Fylde losing at The Athletic Ground 6-29, Bedford being home victors 22-16 and our visitors Moseley going down 21-28.

London Scottish in their home fixture were put to the sword 48-13 then two league games were lost at Brooklands - to Sale 10-21 and at home versus Waterloo 12-16. The Pilkington Cup 2nd round pitted us at home against Sudbury the result a 37-15 win to us. Two visitors, London Irish and Blackheath (league), won 32-15 and 23-13 respectively whilst the third home game, this time in the cup, gave Wakefield the edge 25-22.

December was another month of mixed fortunes with a starting win over Sheffield at Abbeydale Park 15-7 followed by a home loss to Bath 22-38 and a 31-16 home win over London Scottish and, at The Stoop, Harlequins gained the day 34-30.

Again, the second half of the season was better than the first and January saw four wins - over Saracens at home 14-5, away at Coundon Road against Coventry 18-13 in a league game, at home when Askeans gave way 21-51 and, when Middlesborough were visitors, 21-20. The month finished with a home loss to Nottingham 13-20 prior to the cancellation of a match away to Glamorgan Wanderers.

A change of name on the fixture list as Gosforth had now become Newcastle Gosforth and, perhaps because of a new image, they came to us and became victorious 20-9. Sunbury was the venue for our defeat by London Irish 19-18 but weather played its part by forcing Richmond to play the Royal Navy at Roehampton, the honours being even at 23-23.

Gloucester at home were victors 24-15 before we played host to Banca Nationale from Argentina who suffered a 24-55 loss. Back to the league and victory was ours at Scotchgerd Lane by 28-6 over Morley. Hosting again, Richmond entertained another Argentinian side, Lince, and ran up 51 points to the tourists 29. Wakefield visited The Athletic Ground in a League game and gave way 6-11 but the last home game produced a 29-17 win for Leicester. Travelling away for the last two Saturdays resulted in a 29-12 win over Metropolitan Police whilst, in the last league game, Rosslyn Park were winners 24-18.

Our ninth position in National League Two did not save us from the arbitrary league re-organisation and sent us down again to League Three.

Players who appeared most times in the 1st XV were John Allen, John Bower, Paul Carr, Jonathan Clark, Doug Cooper, Phil Della-Savina, Douggie Elliott, Martin Fairn, James Foster, Paul Greenwood, Nick Hawkins, Jason Hoad, Chris Hornung, Mike Hutton, Dean Jeffrey, Howard Lamb, Jonathan Lewis, Martin Livesey, Chris Lloyd, Chris Luxton, Paul McAllister, Adrian McKay, Damian Morris, Simon Pengelly, Rob Ryden, Darryl Sinclair, David Sole, Mark Venner and Matt Yeldham.

The sad death occurred of Tom Rider who was President from 1966 to 1969.

1993/4

The start of the season saw a new team of coaches, following the dismissal of David Hilliard and Kevin Boroevitch from their coaching/captaincy positions. The coaches wer John Kingston, Peter Halsall, Dave Rollitt, Don Taylor, Pat Lavery and, re-appearing, Derek Wyatt.

The season was dominated by a full house of Courage League matches because of the inception of home and away. The President remained Steve James, while Tony Hallett assumed the position of Chairman and Chairman of the Executive Committee, with Alan Skeats restored again to Secretary. Vinny Codrington continued as Director of Rugby.

London Irish and Bedford were both home winners with scores of 21-14 and 23-16 but a short burst of life at home gave Richmond a win against

Sudbury 46-11 before crashing to five defeats, the first three being away to London Welsh 21-23, Wasps 0-34 and Newport 21-29 then at home, in an early dismissal from the Pilkington cup, by Blackheath 21-23 before a first league defeat at Fylde 10-23.

Four more league matches followed, all won, the first three at home with results being Havant 36-3, Redruth 20-9 and Blackheath 22-0, then away at Moseley 27-13. However, the following three league games gave Coventry a 22-15 victory at Richmond followed by another home loss, v Bedford, 12-19 and, in Devon, a win for Exeter 21-16. The last match in December had Harlequins as our visitors and it was a 49-22 home win.

No game was possible on 1st January versus Bath away and a week later Rosslyn Park played away and won 19-6 - (another league loss for us) before we went to Croydon and beat Old Midwhitgiftians 43-6 and then on to Rugby to gain a 20-10 win.

At Hooks Lane, Richmond faced Havant again in the league and lost 16-17 before recording a home win over Fylde 27-25. A trip to Redruth (league) produced a 27-9 win and, at home, Moseley were beaten 34-15 before, at the Rectory Field, Blackheath gained points with an 18-6 win. Metropolitan Police hosted us and lost 0-28 followed by a league success at home versus Morley by 23-10. The league matches with London Scottish at home produced a narrow defeat for us 26-28 and at Coventry we lost 20-33. After Easter, the season finished with a home loss against Bedford 20-26, and two Courage games at Exeter and Rosslyn Park the outcome respectively being a 16-12 win and a 9-36 loss respectively. Final position in National League Three was seventh.

On the field for most of the senior games were Richard Banks, Tim Benson, Paul Carr, Jonathan Clark, David Clift, Andy Cuthbert, Phil Della-Savina, Nana Dontoh, Douggie Elliott, Matt Fitzgerald, James Foster, Giles Goodburn, Paul Greenwood, John Gregory, Jason Hoad, Chris Hornung, Mike Hutton, Dean Jeffreys, Luke Jones, Martin Livesey, Chris Lloyd, Simon Miller, Ed Rowe, Darryl Sinclair, Grant Taylor, Dan Thompson and Matt Yeldham.

1994/5

Steve James continued as President and Tony Hallett continued as Chairman, as did Vinny Codrington as Director of Rugby. Michael Hess became Deputy Chairman and Alistair Law continued as Treasurer. There was a new Secretary, John (Sid) Wright, who brought his scrum-half expertise to us from Nottingham, being voted into the post and the new Captain was Chris Hornung. John Kingston remained in charge of coaching with Peter

Halsall, Dave Rollitt, Don Taylor, Pat Lavery and Martin Fairn (ex Coventry and Richmond).

Three " friendlies" in September were all home matches starting with wins over Reading 13-7 and London Irish 25-13, then a 12-18 loss to Wasps. Harrogate visited Richmond in the league and won 18-6 and the next three league games all meant losses, the victors being Otley at Cross Green Road 19-6, then Bedford visiting us won 16-14 and Clifton at Henbury beat us 18-6.

The league programme was interrupted by a cup 2nd round home tie with Camborne in which the West Country men lost 22-47, but the next three county Courage matches produced no league points as Rugby at home won 21-20, Morley at Richmond scored 38 points to our 17 and, at Roehampton, Rosslyn Park emerged victors 23-21.

Away to Havant in the cup, a victory was registered by Richmond by 15 to 13 then Blackheath in the league came to us and went away 8-3 winners before there was another defeat, this time by London Scottish who outscored us 37-15. December was a month of four victories with defeats inflicted on Newbury 34-18 at Pinchington Lane, home versus London Welsh 27-22, a cancellation v High Wycombe away before a 24-16 win over Tabard at Richmond in the Pilkington Cup 4th round and, finally, a win versus Harlequins 18-13 at The Stoop.

Bad weather caused the abandonment of the first game in January against London Scottish but was followed by two league wins - away at the County Ground, Exeter by a 14-3 margin and against Ottley at home 15-14 before the match with Saracens at Southgate was abandoned after 63 minutes, the score being 10-15 to the home side. Exit from the cup at the end of the month when Northampton sent Richmond packing 15-10 at Franklins Gardens. February was a reasonable month recording a win over Metropolitan Police 68-15 and a league draw away at Headingley on the County Ground 8 points all before Cambridge University were defeated at home 32-7 and, in another league game, Clifton came to us and lost 14-21.

Our return league game at The Athletic Ground with Rugby resulted 19-10 in our favour in March whilst three friendlies beforehand gave us a 16-3 win at home against Northampton, an 18-52 scoreline at Sunbury giving victory to London Irish and, at Scotchard Road, home side Morley were winners by a 31-24 score line.

April began with two Courage matches at home to Rosslyn Park, the result being 14-11 in their favour, and Exeter when the victors were Richmond, scoreline 41-5. The penultimate league match at the Rectory Field Blackheath showed us running out winners 45-9 a week before visitors Newport had their match with us cancelled. Finally, a league visit to Bedford where the result was a narrow loss in the Midlander's favour, by 20-21. At the season's end, Richmond were 8th in the National League Three.

Chris Hornung's leading players of the season were Adrian Boyd, Paul Carr, Dave Clift, Andy Cuthbert, Phil Della-Savina, Nana Dontoh, Matt Dowse, Douggie Elliott, Matt Fitzgerald, James Foster, Giles Goodburn, Paul Greenwood, John Gregory, Jason Hoad, Chris Hornung, Mike Hutton, Jim Kottler, Jonathan Lewis, Chris Lloyd, Dan Luger, Simon Miller, Corin Palmer, Ed Rowe, Geoff Sage, Ben Short, Darren Sinclair, Dan Thompson and Matt Yeldham.

After a period of consistent pressure to keep Richmond's finances healthy, Chairman Tony Hallett had been pleased to announce that the Club's war chest was in rude health with a bank balance of £75,000.

1995/6

In the summer, Tony Hallett, our Chairman for five years, moved on to higher office, to become the Rugby Football Union Secretary and Chief Executive - thus following in the illustrious footsteps of Edward Temple Gurdon.

Steve James gave way as President to David Buchanan, ex Trinity College Dublin and Leinster prop before his glory days with us, who had John Wright as Secretary and Alistair Law as Treasurer with Vinny Codrington as Director of Rugby. The new Chairman was Michael Hess and, on the playing side, Mike (Fat Boy) Hutton took over the captaincy. On the coaching side, under Head Coach John Kingston, were Peter Halsall, Don Taylor, Pat Lavery and Kevan (Dinger) Bell.

The players who supported the Captain in a much better season (we did not lose until November!) were Adrian Boyd, Paul Carr, Jonathan Clarke, Andy Cuthbert, Phil Della-Savina, Dougie Elliott. Matt Fitzgerald, James Foster, Ronan Gavin, Dougie Goodwin, John Gregory, Luke Jones, Jim Kottler, Dan Luger, Corin Palmer, Geoff Sage, Ben Short and Matt Yeldham.

Ten victories in a row started the season - with two friendlies, London Irish (away) 55-28 and Ealing (home) 41-0, followed by Courage victories over Morley (home) 27-24, Rosslyn Park (away) 16-11, Fylde (home) 47-11 and Rotherham at Clifton Lane, 43-6.

October commenced with an away Pilkington Cup Round Two win over Rosslyn Park 22-14 and then three league matches registered a 100% success rate - against Rugby at Webb Ellis Road 21-20, back at home over Otley 46-3 and in Yorkshire 48-19 versus Harrogate. It is believed that ten consecutive wins were the best run in Richmond's history to date. Cup progress was to be limited as our third round draw at Old Deer Park gave London Welsh a 28-18 win followed by a visit to Coventry in the league where the home side out-pointed us 13-12. The rest of the first half of the season was good with only one loss. Blackheath came to Richmond and surrendered league points in losing 15-32 ahead of the only mentioned defeat when London Scottish emerged victors 27-17.

We hosted West London Institute and ran up 66 points to the opponents' 13, travelled to Newbury to win 48-5 but weather stopped our game at Bedford before winning ways again, versus Moseley 32-25 and High Wycombe 53-15 - both at The Athletic Ground, then a weather cancellation against London Welsh away.

Reading at Holme Park was the first Courage game of 1996 and Richmond achieved a narrow 5-3 win, whilst the second league fixture in 1996 saw Rotherham travel to us to lose 9-16. The next home fixture featured Saracens winning by 34-27, but the away game at Cambridge University fell victim to wintry conditions.

Metropolitan Police came to us and surrendered 12-46 but a league game at home with Rugby resulted in an even score of 13-13 prior to a trip north where we gained league points, outscoring Otley 41- 17. Harrogate came to us in the league and lost 7-24 before we welcomed Harlequins but went down 31-36.

Another loss to follow at Northampton, the scoreline being 27-46, whilst, before more league action, the home game with London Scottish produced a 54-29 result to us. Points in the league to be fought for again in the next four Saturdays - two at home against Coventry - score 15-10 to us and Reading - score 28-17, also to us. Morley hosted Richmond and the result was 24-21 in our favour and, when Rosslyn Park came to us, points were gained by Richmond with a final result of 35-26.

Cobden Hill staged the penultimate game against Tabard, the result being a home loss, as we outscored them 41-21, and the final Courage challenge was at Fylde resulting in a victory for the Lancashire side with the scoreline being 26-25.

Final finish in National League Three was first and Richmond were promoted to National League Two.

Away from Richmond, new challenges were emerging for the game - and especially for the RFU, where Tony Hallett was Secretary, in the form of the advent of professionalism, Sky's takeover of the televising of the Five Nations internationals and the emergence of rugby club 'owners'. At Twickenham, he worked with the long ensconced Roger Godfrey (Administrative Secretary of the R.F.U.) an old naval chum and a member of Richmond as he is to this day. He needed all his Naval and Richmond skills to weather the storm. Regrettably the club suffered the passing of our 1966 captain Brian Stoneman.

A momentous change in Rugby Union as, with other leading clubs, Richmond now embraced the professionalism of the game - the age of which is described in a separate chapter - so that, although David Buchanan carried on as President, other administrative duties were fulfilled by salaried persons.

Consequently, the posts of Secretary, Treasurer and Chairman of the Executive disappeared and the running of the club passed to the Chief Executive, Symon Elliott, appointed by new owner, Ashley Levett, with British Lion and England International Ben Clarke captaining the club. John Kingston became Director of Rugby and he had under him Rob Lozowski, the former England and Wasps player, Peter Halsall, Don Taylor and Andy (heinous crime) Maren - well-known as Prosecutor at Richmond's tour courts.

Added to Courage League fixtures were those in the new Anglo-Welsh Cup competition and every game had major significance; no "friendlies" remained.

The team assembled under Ben Clarke included the following - Allan Bateman (Wales), Adrian Boyd, Spencer Brown (RN and subsequently England), Steve Cottrell, Alex Codling, Andy Cuthbert, Adrian Davies (Wales), Jim Fallon, James Foster, Ben Harvey, Luke Jones, Dan McFarland, Simon Mason (Ireland), Andy Moore (Wales), Brian Moore (England), Craig Quinnell (Wales), Scott Quinnell (Wales), Stefan Rodgers, Richard West (England) and Matt Yeldham.

The season now started in August (another tradition gone!) and facing us in the Anglo-Welsh Cup was Maesteg who suffered when Richmond registered the club's then biggest-ever win, 91-3, before playing a league game when Coventry held us to a 16-16 draw at Coundon Road. In two Courage League matches, Rotherham went down 38-64 at The Athletic Ground whilst, at Bedford, the home side capitulated 17-44 , before we travelled to The Reddings to meet Moseley in the same competition to come back 87-15 victors.

Three more Courage matches notched up a lot more points as London Scottish were defeated 54-13 and Rugby 64-8, both at home, whilst travel to Blackheath saw a 40-21 win in Richmond's favour. Sixty four points to thirteen was our league score at home over Waterloo and, in away fixtures (also league), Wakefield 23-7 and Nottingham 70-5 were seen off.

The intended fixture with Combined Services at Richmond was cancelled but then back to winning ways beating Tabard 58-21 at home in a friendly and a 71-14 thrashing of visitors Pontypool in the Anglo-Welsh Competition before, at home, Cross Keys gave us best 17-27 in the same tournament.

Two non-competitive (as such) matches, both at Richmond, gave welcome visitors Western Samoa a clear 32-12 victory after which London Welsh conceded 64 points to our 12. Pilkington Cup Round Five proved a reverse as, in Lancashire, Sale proceeded to the next round 34-30 - but back to winning ways at the end of the year hosting Coventry and scoring a 39-10 win.

A weather-stricken January with opening Courage games away at Rotherham and at home versus Bedford falling to icy conditions before Newport were beaten 29-17 in a non-competitive game at Rodney Parade and then climatic conditions forced a postponement of the league game at Newcastle. To play the earlier postponed match Bedford visited us and lost 33-34 before weather closed in again and Richmond could not travel to Bath.

A Courage League home game gave us victory over Moseley 37-27 before we had the pleasure of welcoming Otago from New Zealand - the result being a thrashing - we lost 0-70. Clifton Lane in Rotherham gave us a 28-3 victory and, three days later, the Royal Navy were Richmond's guests, losing 12-60 in one of the few friendlies.

All other games in the season were part of both tournaments being noted as C (Courage) and AW (Anglo-Welsh) and the outcomes were Cross Keys (AW) a home win 58-7, a home win 37-18 v London Scottish (C); Maesteg (away, AW) was cancelled, Rugby (away C) was a splendid 72-31 win for Richmond; Newcastle (away, C) we lost 17-31, Blackheath (home, C) win to us 29-24, Waterloo (away, C) the home side lost 29-58; Wakefield (home, C) our victory 55-22, and finally Nottingham (home C) yielded to us 0-34. This year saw another dramatic league success, with successive championships seeing Richmond's promotion to National League One (later re-named The Premiership) - a first in the club's history.

Scott Quinnell, Alan Bateman and new signing, Barry Williams, were selected for the Lions Tour to South Africa.

1997/8

David Buchanan again took over the helm as President with Symon Elliott being Chief Executive and John Kingston overseeing playing matters as Director of Rugby. The position of General Manager was taken by Peter Moore, our old full back and originally a player with Waterloo, and Ben Clarke remained as Captain. Under John Kingston, coaches were Rob Lozowski, Don Taylor, Kevan Bell, Peter Halsall, Andy Maren and Mark Tainton (the kicking coach from Bath).

The club embarked on an early season August tour of Ireland which brought three wins - against Lansdowne, Ulster and Greystones before meeting London Scottish in a friendly won by us. The first league game, now sponsored by Allied Dunbar, against London Irish resulted in a home win for

Richmond 32-12 and August ended with a postponed league game versus Saracens away.

Apart from the league, Richmond were involved also in the European Conference, the opening match of which meant a trip to Colomiers which was lost 18-34 preceding two more home games in the same tournament when we recorded 43-11 and 37-8 victories against Bridgend and Grenoble. Away at Bridgend, the result was 44-72 in favour of Richmond and away again at Grenoble the winning margin was 29-16 to us. Saracens were faced away to complete the postponed game but we crashed 9-15 before travelling to Colomiers where the French side outscored us 49-25.

Then back to the league at home when Harlequins were defeated 37-16 but a visit to Newcastle saw us give best to the northern side 9-18. Richmond had reached the quarterfinal of the European Conference but were to go no further as Bath beat us 47-31. A welcome relaxation from competition brought New South Wales to visit us and a 43-24 win over them was registered.

Yet another competition had been instigated, 'the League Cup', and at home London Scottish were overcome 30-7 as were Blackheath 31-8 but then we failed, losing 17-27 to Bedford at home. Back to league fixtures and Bristol came to us and returned 12-13 losers before we achieved a rare victory over Leicester, at home, 32-15. The year finished with three league losses - at home to Northampton 21-24 and two away, to Gloucester 26-29 and Wasps 18-22.

The Pilkington Cup was still in evidence and, in January in the 4th round playing at home, Richmond overcame Doncaster 58-8 but January weather being what it is meant that the league game with Bath was postponed. The league game away at London Irish was a triumphant victory for Richmond by 45-14 followed by a Pilkington Cup win at home versus Bath, the score being 29-14. In the league, Saracens visited Richmond and won 15-10, then a league cup match with Cambridge University gave us a 63-38 victory. Sale were faced in the league at home and the visitors returned to Lancashire with a 28-20 victory in advance of two quarter-finals when, in the League Cup at Kingsholm, Gloucester emerged winners by 39-27 and, in the Pilkington Cup, Saracens travelled and took away the spoils 36-30.

Back to the league and at The Stoop, the home team Harlequins placed a 41-12 win in the frame but, in the following league fixture at Majedski Stadium, our new home ground in Reading, Newcastle went home empty-handed having lost 17-30. Leicester at home scored 42 points to our 19 in another league game.

Only league games were now left with the winning results being versus Bristol (home) 43-3, Bath (home) 32-14, Northampton (away) 47-39, Gloucester (home) 33-22 and Wasps (home) 51-29. The final position for the

Richmond in the Premiership was fifth - arguably the highest definitive 'ranking' the club had achieved in its long history.

The team photograph indicated that the prominent players of the season were Allan Bateman, Spencer Brown, Paul Carr, Dominic Chapman, Steve Cottrell, Darren Crompton, Andy Cuthbert, Adrian Davies, John Davies, Mel Deane, Matthew Fitzgerald, James Foster, Craig Gillies, Ben Harvey, Mike Hutton, Robbie Hutton, Ben Leigh, Dan McFarland, Rolando Martin, Simon Mason, Andy Moore, Corin Palmer, Agustin Pichot, Matthew Pini, Craig Quinnell, Scott Quinnell, Earl Va'a, Adam Vander, Richard West, Barry Williams and Jason Wright.

A sad occasion for the club, as Bill Munks the 1960 and 1961 Captain was laid to rest in his beloved Sussex, and Sir John Megaw, our President from 1951 to 1954, also passed on.

1998/9

A new President in Tony Dorman, a longstanding member and an Old Cranleighan - John Kingston and Ben Clarke retained their roles as Director of Rugby and Captain respectively. Symon Elliott had disappeared from the scene but Peter Moore was still General Manager and assumed the role of Company Secretary with Tony Hallett, as Chief Executive in succession to Symon, leading the Board of Directors (Tony Hallett had resigned from the RFU in 1998 following a public disagreement with the RFU Chairman concerning the integrity of the game which Tony considered was being usurped and mismanaged).

Three competitions existed viz. The National (Allied Dunbar) League, the C & G League Cup and the Tetley Cup.

September kicked off with a victory at home over Newcastle but Gloucester visited us and returned home 25-22 winners before we lost away to Bath 14-26. The last home fixture of the month showed a 28-13 win over Swansea.

October was good as, at Sunbury, London Irish lost to us 29-33 and at home we had the better of West Hartlepool 41-23 before, away on a Sunday at Wasps, the score was 27-22 in our favour. Leicester at home are virtually unbeatable and so it proved as they scored 27 to our nothing, then at Sale we won 39-10.

On the first Sunday in November at home we beat Bedford 38-22 but then lost away to Saracens 17-33 before we went down 27-44 away to Northampton. We beat London Welsh in the C & G Cup at home 26-10 but, before the return match a week later, we withdrew from the competition.

Three matches in December with results being Cardiff at home, a win for us 35-28 followed by an away victory over London Scottish 28-6 but a home reverse against London Irish 13-25.

Starting the New Year, Swansea were faced at St Helens - result a 3-57 beating and then, in an evening kick-off at home, visitors Leicester won 23-11. In the Tetley Cup, we welcomed Newbury and had a 45-12 victory and then we shared the spoils 24-25 away to Gloucester. Two victories came next with scores of 40-22 over London Scottish and over Exeter in the Tetley Cup 37-10, both at home.

The match with Newcastle was postponed so only two games were played in February - at home to Sale who we beat 29-24 and also at home to Leicester (Tetley Cup), a match we won 15-13. Only three matches occurred in March when we lost at home to Bath 23-30, drew away with Harlequins 32-32 and travelled to the north east where West Hartlepool kept Richmond down to a one point win in the 35-36 result.

Then came the rearranged fixture with Newcastle (away) and we suffered a 14-47 loss followed by another dismal result when we went down at home to Wasps 5-29. We were now into May with a 25/75% outcome as we lost to Harlequins 23-30 at The Athletic Ground, were beaten again at home by Northampton 19-31 before another home game gave Saracens the edge as we lost 18-25. The season ended on the most resounding note when at Bedford, Richmond registered the clubs highest score ever - a colossal 106-12 scorecard to bring a traumatic period to a triumphant end, resulting in the club finishing ninth in the National League.

By now the events described in detail in Chapter 12 were in full flow, resulting in Richmond being rejected from the Premiership without justification and with the sanction of the Premiership Chairman, best forgotten, Tom Walkinshaw, and condemned by a leaderless RFU and unsupportive Middlesex (our county!). The players and club members bade a sad but somehow triumphant farewell to an exciting and, in playing terms, successful era.

1st XV players who figured in the squad were Alan Bateman, Lee Best, Spencer Brown, Laurent Cabannes, Dominic Chapman, Alex Codling, Darren Crompton, Brian Cusack, Andy Cuthbert, Adrian Davies, John Davies, Mel Deane, Matt Dixon, Maurice Fitzgerald, Craig Gillies, Jim Hamilton-Smith, Robbie Hutton, Dan Macfarland, Andy Moore, Corin Palmer, Agustin Pichot, Matt Pini, Craig Quinell, Scott Quinnell, Brian Shelbourne, Earl Va'a, Adam Vander, Nick Warne, Tom Whitford, Barry Williams, and Jason Wright.

Regrettably, another sad death, this time of Fred Stoy who was President 1978 - 1981.

In the professional era, Richmond were honoured by the award of International caps to the following players - Rolando Martin, Agustin Pichot

(Argentina), Spencer Brown, Dominic Chapman, Ben Clarke (England), Allan Bateman, Craig Quinnell, Scott Quinnell, Nick Walne, Barry Williams (Wales), Simon Mason (Ireland), Matt Pini (Italy), Earl Va'a (Western Samoa).

1999/2000

Although Richmond had departed from the professional scene as recorded in a separate chapter, Tony Dorman remained as President with Tony Hallett resuming the role of Chairman of the Executive, renamed the Management Committee, leading Simon Everton as Secretary and Neil Aitken as Treasurer. Kevan (Dinger) Bell took over as Director of Rugby and Captaincy was in the hands of Andy Cuthbert. Senior Squad coaches were Peter Halsall and Andy Maren.

In spite of RFU's earlier promises to place Richmond in a meaningful league, opposition was encountered from our Constituent Body, Middlesex, and the club was required to take a 'sabbatical' season, facing a season of friendlies with the hope that good results would prove Richmond's ability to face opponents of stern quality in "an appropriate league" as indicated by R.F.U. officials. The sterling efforts of the Fixture Secretary Vic Balchin produced a meaningful fixture list, which resulted in a good season.

The season began in late September when visitors Old Colfeians lost 13-18 before we beat the 2nd XV of national league side Henley away 39-26 and then came a home beating of London Irish amateurs 58-8. London Kiwis came to The Athletic Ground and took the spoils 19-13 before an away match with Cambridge University was cancelled.

Having successfully seen off the marauding intents of the Administrators, the penultimate match in October featured a Launch Day of the revitalised club with the 1st XV facing the President's XV who were outwitted by a score of 31-23, then Newbury travelled to us and lost 15-27. An away game at Ruislip gave Richmond the edge 15-12; Rosslyn Park 2nd XV at home scored 31 to our 5 but another match with them was cancelled and December was bare of fixtures.

In January two wins followed - over R.M.A Sandhurst at home 56-12 and, against another national league side 2nd XV, Richmond outscored Bracknell 38-17 on their ground.

London Welsh 2nd XV were not so kind to us at Old Deer Park and they won 29-8 but Harlow were beaten 30-5 in Essex. Then away to Reading I but Richmond went down 29-35 - not bad against a national league XV, followed by meeting another national league second fifteen on our ground, this time Camberley, who had their ears clipped 63-6. Rosslyn Park 2nd XV came to us and repeated their earlier win, this time with a winning margin 41-14.

Tabard were next tackled at home and we won 31-19; the Royal Navy fixture was cancelled so Richmond followed with a conclusive 33-3 win over London Irish amateurs on their pitch before Rosslyn Park Emerging XV came to us and went back 28-12 winners. Blackheath (another national league side) suffered at our hands at The Athletic Ground to the tune of 50-10, in the oldest fixture between any two sides in the world.

At home again, we entertained London Kiwis who bested us 31-10 and the season wound up with cancelled matches versus Basingstoke and Henley II before St Just visited The Athletic Ground and lost 5-55.

Chapter Five

The First Five Years of the New Millennium

2000/01

The Rugby Football Union, having noted our previous successful "friendly" season, reneged on its assurance of "an appropriate league position" and connived with Middlesex C.R.F.U. to place the club in Hertfordshire and Middlesex Division I even though, as a result of the support we had received from Surrey C.R.F.U., our allegiance had been transferred to that county.

Overseeing this transfer of allegiance was President Tony Dorman with Tony Hallett at his elbow as Chairman. Andrew Gordon became Secretary and General Manager with Neil Aitkien keeping his role as Treasurer and Peter Moore and David Corben as directors. On the playing side, Andy Cuthbert stayed as Captain and Kevan Bell as Director of Rugby, but he left during the season and Andy Maren, Head of Coaching, took over.

Apart from the league situation, Richmond were also to be involved in the Intermediate and Surrey Cups and a tremendous season realised only two losses with a fantastic points advantage never before achieved in the whole history of the club.

Ealing were entertained in the opening game and lost 10-20 to be followed by an Intermediate Cup-tie away at Guildfordians resulting in victory 50-0. The opening league game saw co-tenants London Scottish at home edge a 15-11 win, but welcoming Old Hamptonians in the league our points were 33 to their 17. Travel in the league to Stevenage achieved a 67-8 triumph before an Intermediate Cup match with Grasshoppers at home shattered our visitors 61-10.

League games; first at home, next two away, produced points galore as Richmond ran up scores of 36-7 against Feltham, 45-0 over Lensbury and 62-0 in opposition to Mill Hill. November brought another Intermediate Cup match when travel was made to Winchester who succumbed 0-39 before, in torrential rain in the league at Enfield, the Ignations were overcome 31-0. Uxbridge away were the next league fixture but they too failed to score as we ran in 56 points.

The Intermediate Cup again and old rivals Sudbury were defeated 52-0 at Richmond before, during December, the game versus London Welsh at home was cancelled and league wins were recorded against Harrow 40-0 and Enfield Ignations 73-3, both at home.

January took Richmond into the Intermediate Cup again and the tie when Tunbridge Wells came to us resulted in another win, this time 23-13. This month visitors Mill Hill gave best to the club 71-0 and, after a postponement versus Lensbury, the next round of the Intermediate Cup brought Gloucestershire side Thornbury to us but they returned empty handed having lost 5-34.

Another change of competition meant a Surrey Cup game when Guildford and Godalming came to us and went away 0-25 losers and, at home again, Richmond overcame Stevenage 68-0 in the league.

The abandoned game against Lensbury took place when our visitors lost 0-41 then back to the Intermediate Cup when Sheffield were our visitors but suffered 17-25. The home Surrey Cup semi-final against London Irish Amateurs gave Richmond a 35-9 win followed by a revenge win in the league 13-5 over London Scottish -we were the hosts.

Then a long trip to Newcastle to meet Blaydon in the semi-final of the Intermediate Cup and the Geordies emerged winners 22-10; incidentally, they lost the Final but got promoted to National League Three North.

The next outing was to Harrow to win 30-7 before Uxbridge came to Richmond and scored five points whilst we registered 84. The last three games featured the Surrey Cup Final when Dorking scored 10 but could not match Richmond's 35 and two re-arranged league games both away when Feltham 5-63 and Old Hamptonians 0-29 were the losers. This meant that Richmond had won the league and gained promotion having scored 853 points with only 72 against.

Getting amongst the phenomenal points scored - all the matches in the Intermediate Cup were against clubs leagues above us - were the following players in the squad - Rupert Allhusen, Ade Bamford, Stewart Barlow, Andrew Beacham, Oliver Bishop, Martin Bolton, Richard Bragg, Matt Brown, Alister Burns, Jim Darragh, Alex Davey, Matt Dunn, Ean Evans, James Evans, Ross Evans, Sean Flynn, Leigh Hancock, Henry Head, Rob Kenworthy, Jim Kottler, Ben Leigh, Dom Little, Simon Lodder, John Macey, Gareth Neal, Steve Nock, Corin Palmer, Tom Price, Jim Samuel, Pieter Serfontein, Will Taylor, Damian Walker, Andy Warne, Chris Whiteley, Paul Wilson and James Woods.

The Club was also honoured by Andy Cuthbert's selection for the Barbarians.

Richmond suffered three sad blows in the passing of Johnny Williams (Captain 1954-56), Ken Morley, who had earlier coached us so well and Dr Tom Roberts who gave many years' service as the Club's doctor.

2001/2

A new President emerged with Ian Botes, a veteran club member and a mighty prop who had captained the Heavies, taking the post whilst Andrew Gordon remained as Secretary. The team of Tony Hallett (Chairman), Neil Aitken (Treasurer) and Andy Cuthbert (Captain) were re-elected and, under a new title, Andy Maren became Head of Coaching. Management Committee appointments were: David Corben (Marketing), Peter Moore (Financial Director), Andrew Gordon (Secretary), Andy Quigley (Chairman Playing) and Harry Hooper (Media).

Promotion having been achieved, the club was now to play in London IV South West League and would enter the Surrey Cup as holders. Games would be played also in the Intermediate Cup - at our behest. The club found itself in an extraordinary position as the RFU rejected our case for elevation to a higher league but, nevertheless, argued that, following last season's success in the Intermediate Cup, Richmond should be entered in the premier cup competition. So they wanted it both ways - with non-enhancement of our league position (except for the one league gained via promotion) but with the intention to place us in with the "big boys" in the cup. We stuck to our guns and so remained at the intermediate level.

The first game was a friendly with Esher II when we registered a 41-0 win at home before travelling to US Portsmouth for the first league game where Richmond ran out victors 71-6. The home league match against Cranleigh produced a 107-3 score-line in our favour but Warlingham withdrew from the next league game at The Athletic Ground and we entertained Wimbledon who returned to SW19 the losers 0-42.

Barnes - a strong side - entertained us but lost 19-44 at Barn Elms Park and away again, also in the league, a below-standard performance at Old Emmanuel nevertheless gave us a 24-7 win. In the league Tottonians visited Richmond but their 10 points could not match our 69. The first round of the Intermediate Cup brought a 83-5 home win against Law Society but then back to the league when Old Reedonians at home gave way to us 0-67. The next league opponents, Warlingham, cried off and Bracknell II stepped into the breach but to no advantage as they lost 16-25 at Richmond.

Points were still rattling up and our Intermediate Cup opponents, New Milton, came to us and went away empty-handed having lost 5-79, which was followed by an away trip to Farnborough where we amassed a 50-10 scoreline. Farnham travelled to Richmond and lost 3-50 a week before we took on Canterbury in the cathedral city when Thomas A'Beckett failed to turn up - so we won 38-14 against another club leagues above us.

December brought a wet visit to Purley John Fisher and, again, the score was a rout in our favour 58-12 before, a week later, Trojans visited us and also suffered a mauling by 3-58. Next opponents in the Intermediate Cup were Sutton and Epsom - they surrendered 9-20.

At the end of the month and in the first week of January, weather caused the postponement of league games away to Farnham and at home to Farnborough. On resumption of fixtures Warlingham entertained us but we spurned their hospitality by winning 58-0. The next weekend was going to be tough with two games in two days; firstly at home versus Diss in the Intermediate Cup and then away to Old Mid-Whitgiftians in the Surrey Cup. Richmond were up to both challenges and respectively won 34-3 and, in atrocious conditions, 12-3.

Back at home, we played Old Reedonians in the league and superior fitness wore down early spirited opposition and the result was 51-0 in Richmond's favour, then an away trip to Tottonians produced a very competitive game with the result, 25-10 to Richmond, only determined in the final quarter of the match.

In a cup draw behind closed doors at RFU Twickenham with no club officials invited, we were pitched away in the Intermediate Cup to Halifax - another club four leagues above us. In very blustery conditions Halifax shot to a 13-0 lead after some ten minutes but the tenacious play of Richmond got us to within one point at the final whistle, the score being 20-19 in the host's favour. Halifax later won the cup and celebrated their victory at RFU Twickenham in fine style at our clubhouse.

Another cup-tie a week later when University Vandals were faced in the Surrey Cup quarter final at Walton. Although the opposition played spiritedly, it was really one-way traffic and Richmond ran in a 52-3 victory consisting of ten tries but only one conversion.

The then current league leaders (having played more games then us) Barnes were our visitors but crumpled in the first half conceding nineteen points. The second half brought order back into their game and, with a poor Richmond performance, they got back to 12-19 but the match ended at that score to ensure that we went to the head of the table. The re-arranged match with Farnham, played on a muddy, sloping (every way) pitch, produced a fine 30-3 win.

On a normal field the following week at Cranleigh, the match ended conclusively in our favour 50-12 (after a slow start) but we struggled at home against an improved U.S Portsmouth XV but ran out winners 24-0. At Browns Lane, Effingham and Leatherhead, coached by a former Richmond player Simon Dear, faced us in the semi-final of the Surrey Cup and, after trailing early on by 0-11, our game was raised and produced a 35-11 win.

Then back to the league and a journey to Southampton to meet Trojans but, unfortunately, they did not come out of their horse and we romped away with a

101-0 victory and the game was blown up five minutes early! Next victims were Purley John Fisher who visited Richmond and went away ruing a 5-84 defeat.

And so to defend the Surrey Cup with a Final at Esher against Sutton & Epsom which proved to be a nail biter. Richmond having gone to 13-0 at the interval found that the opposition refused to lie down and crept back to 11-13 but their conversion attempt in the last minute failed. So Surrey's prime trophy was ours for a second year.

The penultimate match was the re-arranged one against a plucky Old Emmanuel XV who had no answer to our game plan and lost 0-102.

Promotion had been achieved with a 100% record and a points difference of over one thousand - so on to London III S.W.

Andy Cuthbert's most regular support came from, in desending order of appearances, Ross Evans, Simon Lodder, Henry Head, Antony Phillips, Sean Flynn, Mike McSweeney, Rupert Allhusen, Will Taylor, Chris Whiteley, Matt Yeldham, Ollie Quigley, Andy Warne, Arthur Irving, Martin Bolton, Stewart barlow, James (Tigger) Woods, Matt Brown, Tom Price, Ben Leigh, Mark Draper, Jim Samuel, Pieter Serfontein, Mike Hull, Paul Wilson, Jim Kottler, Jim Darragh, Dan Taberner, Paul Harrison, Zoran Higgins, Andy Beacham, Oli Bishop, James Evans, Steve Nock, Nick Hawkins, Dom Little, Alan Brown and Alfie Ambrose.

Andy Cuthbert added more Barbarians caps to his wardrobe - a fitting reward for a man who has given his all for the game. Sadly the season saw the passing of Graham Tardif, our President in 1989-92.

2002/3

The personnel at the top of the club remained in their posts as last year and all were keen to take us forward in London League III SW to greater glory and so it was to prove that way.

The season commenced at the end of August with a home game in the Powergen Senior Cup against Gosport & Fareham resulting in a comprehensive victory by 64-0 which meant travelling to Clifton for the next round to play a National League III South team who crumpled to a 14-66 loss against Richmond.

Week three of the season was the date for the first league game when a sixty nine points to nil thrashing was handed out to Old Wimbledonians at home but our Cup run ended a week later. We were drawn against Westcombe Park and their higher league status showed as they came to The Athletic Ground and won 31-20.

Back to league games with an away game at Walton v University Vandals who were stopped in their tracks by 13-53 followed by a visit to The Athletic

Ground by Old Blues who were also on a large defeat by 7-58.

A very large contingent of supporters emerged the following week to take advantage of the luxury of a game in Jersey and they were pleased, not just by the good weather and fine hotels but by a clear-cut 32-3 win after a nail-biting first half hour. Following our demise in the Cup, Richmond were fortunate to pick up a friendly game, away against League III South Reading, but their higher status was demolished as Richmond won 35-12.

Then through to the middle of December six league games were played the results of which were Guildford (home) 67-7, Dorking (away) 58-10, Chobham (home) 50-0, Barnes (away) 22-10, Alton (home) 83-3 and Chobham (away) 27-7 - all Richmond victories.

Resuming in the New Year, we faced Dorking at home and ran in seventy-seven points to their three but then bad weather stopped our friendly v London Scottish before travel to Guildford for a league fixture gave us another win, by 41-0.

Our first outing in the Surrey Cup produced a home match against Esher II who were seen off 38-3 and then back to league games when Jersey, our visitors, were beaten 30-13 and, at Old Blues' ground in Raynes Park, we ran in seventy four points to the home side's eleven.

The Quarter-Final of the Surrey Cup meant a home fixture against Dorking who failed to score against Richmond's 63 points and then, at home, University Vandals were put to the sword 49-0. Time for the Surrey Cup Semi-Final when Rosslyn Park II were our visitors - but they travelled back to Roehampton losers by a score of 10-29.

Old Wimbledonians hosted us in the league but lost 3-42 before a home friendly versus Old Mid-Whitgiftians gave Richmond an 18-3 win and then an away league game at Alton produced a 32-0 victory. At Imber Court, Surrey CRFU staged their Cup-Final and we again played Sutton & Epsom and, after a tense game, took the top honour for the third year in succession by a score of 27-18. On to the last league match against Barnes at home and a tough game just gave us the edge 20-15.

Supporting Andy Cuthbert in yet another record-breaking year were: Rupert Allhusen, Stewart Barlow, Matt Brown, Chris Conway, Nana Dontoh, Arthur Irving, Ben Leigh, Simon Lodder, Alex Maclennan, Mike McSweeney, Anthony Phillips, Tom Price, Ollie Quigley, Pieter Serfontein, John Schofield, Dan Taberner, Will Taylor, Richard Thomas, Andy Warne, Chris Whiteley, James Whitfield, Paul Wilson, Matt Wooderson, Matt Yeldham.

2003/4

For a third year running all the top positions of the club remained in the same very capable hands who produced, on and off the pitch, another highly successful season by gaining promotion (yet again), this time to London 1 and by producing very sound financial performance.

A training game in August against our old friends Blackheath produced a win ahead of the first match in the Powergen Cup which brought Jersey to The Athletic Ground where they were despatched 85-3. That result meant Richmond were drawn at home in the next round to Canterbury and nail-biting spectators saw us scrape through 12-11 before we got back to the form of previous years by starting the league programme with a 48-5 home win against Chobham.

Back to the Powergen Cup and an away fixture at Haywards Heath where a club in the league above us were seen off 31-17 before travelling away again, this time in the league, brought a 39-8 victory at Sidcup.

With the Powergen Cup now being a national as opposed to earlier round regional basis, Richmond had to travel to Wakefield where, after holding our own for forty five minutes against the National League 2 side we succumbed in the second half and lost out 20-48.

The remaining two matches in October produced a return to form in the league away at Winchester by a 75-5 margin but then we fell away in a friendly against London Welsh II who returned to Old Deer Park as winners.

November saw four league games, all of which provided substantial victories running up nearly two hundred points as the club demolished Beckenham away 48-3, Tunbridge Wells at home 43-8, Portsmouth away in a storm tossed match 75-17 and close rivals Barnes at The Athletic Ground 27-0.

A visit to Andover in December resulted in a forty points to three victory followed by another league game (re-arranged because of earlier Powergen Cup success) at Wimbledon where the home XV failed to move against Richmond's 34 points. Portsmouth came to visit us in the league but returned to Hampshire having lost 10-65.

Five league matches in January saw no end to the winning vein and five clubs which were put to the sword were Tunbridge Wells 39-15 in Kent, Beckenham at Richmond 36-7, Old Mid-Whitgiftians also at home 63-3, Gosport & Fareham, playing at the Naval Base as their clubhouse was being refurbished, 42-15, and then Winchester at our ground by a 37-12 margin.

We were not required to enter the early rounds of the Surrey Cup but had a tie against Sutton & Epsom away at the beginning of February who we beat more comprehensively than the year earlier - this time it was 41-3. Back to

71

league games in the same month and more big wins - at Old Mid-Whitgiftians the score in our favour being 38-19 then at home to Sidcup when the Kent side scored one penalty goal to counter our 72 points. The month finished by demolishing Cobham away by 82 points to 10.

March brought the semi-final of the Surrey Cup when the club travelled to meet Guildford & Godalming and progressed to the final by winning 34-18. Wimbledon came to Richmond for a league match but lost 3-43 before, a fortnight later, we faced Esher II at their ground in the Surrey Cup final and, yet again, we took the trophy, this time by a 30-14 margin.

The penultimate league game versus Andover at home gave us the points but not a proper score as the Hampshire side did not turn up. Finally, in mid-April, we took on Barnes at Barn Elms and ensured our leadership of the league by achieving a 34-9 victory.

The most used players were: Rupert Allhusen, Ade Bamford, Stewart Barlow, Matt Brown, Steve Dixon, Peter Enright, Ross Evans, Andy Greally, Owen Gregory, Lewis Gunn, Ed Hallett, Henry Head, Vince Holden, Tom Hood, Dylan James, Ben Leigh, Alex Maclennan, Mike McSweeney, Neil Piggot, John Schofield, Martin Slattery, Tom Stokes, Dan Taberner, Richard Thomas, Harvey Thorneycroft, Chris Whiteley, James Whitfield, Paul Wilson.

As the outgoing President Ian Botes wrote in Goalposts "The 1st Team bandwagon rolls on and remains unbeaten after 79 consecutive league wins - add that to four consecutive Surrey Cup wins and you have a truly outstanding performance." Strangely, Ian omitted to mention that the number of league wins in a row is a national record!

Mention should be made also of the Development XV which came second in London Merit Table A and the Saxons - second in London Merit Table B whilst the Vikings won the Lambs Cup.

2004/5

Changes at the top of the club meant that, after an impressive three years, Ian Botes stood down as President in favour of Tony Hallett whose position as Chairman was taken by David Corben. Andrew Gordon continued as Secretary and Jen Gadsby Peet as Assistant Treasurer - but no mention of a Treasurer in the Fixture/Membership Card. All other senior positions remained in the same safe hands, especially those of captain Andy Cuthbert who alleges that his safe pair of hands mean he should be playing as a back.

After a practice match at home with Blackheath, the real season started, as is the norm now, with a Powergen Cup match away at Thurrock but the home XV could not resist us and went down 7-73. On to the next cup round when we faced Old Colfeians at The Athletic Ground and progressed by winning 51-0.

So to the first league game at home against demoted Basingstoke and another win by a narrower margin than usual, 18-7, followed by a Powergen Cup game against Southend of National III South, won only in the last minutes by twenty-two to twenty points. However, the end of September saw a return to large scores when, away at Nackington Road, the home side Canterbury went down 10-50.

Cup action again, this time against National League III South side Hertford who could not match Richmond and lost 7-31, before travel to London Nigerians brought another league win by 24-14. Further progress in the Cup was halted by National League III North side Kendal who travelled from the Lake District and took the spoils 18-13.

For the last two Saturdays of October it was league action and a home 46-13 trouncing of Thanet Wanderers proved to be the last of Richmond's world record breaking run of eighty three successive league victories for, a week later at high-flying Worthing, the home side outscored us by 24-20.

Then a second disaster struck a week later when a visit to Bishop's Stortford brought another defeat this time by an 8-24 score line. With all being up for grabs at the top of the table, we then achieved three handsome victories - over Cambridge at home 36-5, Sutton & Epsom away 28-6 and Old Colfeians at home 45-15.

So to the great meeting with our tenants London Scottish but three thousand spectators witnessed a third league defeat for Richmond who capitulated by fifteen points to twenty three. To get that loss out of our system, we hammered visitors Sutton & Epsom the following week 41-0 before travelling to Cambridge where recent poor form was to the fore and our East Anglian rivals revelled in a 27-12 victory. So, in the promotion race, a month or so had seen Richmond drop from being a leading contender to the position of an also-ran.

The knife in the wound was thrust harder two weeks later when Worthing visited The Athletic Ground and returned to Sussex victors by 17 points to 15. January ended with a thirty eight points to twelve win over ThanetWanderers away and, on the first Saturday in February, London Nigerians were our visitors but went back home empty handed having lost 8-31.

Richmond entertained Old Albanians and won comfortably 29-10 but, when we visited the same opponents a week later, the home side achieved revenge by an 18 points to 5 margin. February finished with a thirty three points to nil victory over Canterbury at The Athletic Ground.

Travelling to Hampshire to play Basingstoke brought a 42-27 win but, unfortunately, our rivals for promotion, principally Cambridge, Worthing and London Scottish, had lost fewer games and were winning by larger margins than Richmond, so yet another promotion was looking extremely doubtful.

Meanwhile, nothing had happened in the Surrey Cup as our Quarter-Final fixture was cancelled as Sutton & Epsom cried off so the club had a fortnight's break before we revenged ourselves over Bishop's Stortford at home to the tune of 41-12. A week later further revenge was achieved when Richmond posted a 15-3 victory over London Scottish.

The club's grip on the Surrey Cup came to an end when, in a nail-biting finish, a scoreline of 18-16 gave Rosslyn Park II the edge. The season finished with an away league game against Old Colfeians and this was a win for Richmond 25-15 which meant that the club finished in third place in London I, promotion hopes having been dashed by the defeats in October and November. Cambridge won the league and Worthing, in second place, failed to win a play-off for a place in Division III South.

Leading players of the season were: Joseph Ajuwa, Stewart Barlow, Matt Brown, Don Connolly, Steve Dixon, Ross Evans, Jonathan Farmer, Nick Gaskell, Owen Gregory, Lewis Gunn, Ed Hallett, Simon Hallett, Tom Hood, Dave Ingham, Andy Lee, Ben Leigh, Simon Lodder, Alex Maclennan, Cathal Murphy, Tim O'Shea, Neil Piggot, Andy Saunders, Tom Stokes, Dan Taberner, Richard Thomas, James Whitfield, Paul Wilson.

2005/6

All the top officials retained their positions with Richard (Touchjudge) Humphrey assuming the role of Director of Rugby. Andy Cuthbert stood down after years of sterling service as Captain but assumed the role of Club Captain and the new 1st XV skipper was Dan Taberner. However, the Cuthbert name was still held in high regard in the shape of Michelle who continued her excellent service as Senior Physio.

After the disappointment of missing out on promotion in the previous season, Richmond continued in London League Division 1 with another daunting season ahead as it was known that some rival clubs were now operating on a semi-professional basis.

The opening match was away in Hanworth against Staines in a National Trophy match and a clear 50-13 win was achieved. So to the first league fixture and a journey to Tabard in Radlett resulted in a 60-21 victory for us. Back to the National Trophy where we fell at this hurdle against Ealing who won convincingly by 38 points to 22.

Cup matches, except for the Surrey Cup later in the season, were now over so time to concentrate on league matches with the XV bolstered by the presence of Bob Skinstad - the former South African International captain now living in London.

A home tie v Bishop's Stortford gave Richmond the advantage 46-11, followed by an away win by 31-19 over Old Albanians and then revenge against Ealing at The Athletic Ground with a 32-12 scoreline. October finished when Richmond travelled to Worthing, always a high-flying XV, but returned home as 26-19 victors and then scored 16 points to Staines 3 at home.

Only two matches were played in November - the other Saturdays being Cup days in which we had no interest and these resulted in full league points with important wins over Canterbury away, 24-17, and Barnes at home, 31-13.

December was very successful when the club racked up 117 points by way of beating Old Colfeians away 60-3, London Scottish at home 27-25 and Barnes at Barn Elms to the tune of 30-18. The match against our Athletic Ground co-tenants was an amazing affair as we played the entire second half with only fourteen men following a red card incident but the side was inspired by our South African star and held on for a nailbiting victory.

Richmond had now had a run of ten victories but the New Year brought no joy as Canterbury visited us and inflicted a defeat by 18-15 and, although this was followed by a 39-34 win at Staines, another defeat was to follow. This was at home by 25-26 against Worthing and we then entered the Surrey Cup at the Quarter-final stage at Esher where the home side's Cardinals narrowly won 20-15. However, it was established that our opponents had fielded three unqualified players so they forfeited their victory, enabling Richmond to proceed to the Semi-final.

So back to league matches, the first of which was another loss when, travelling to Ealing, we could only score twenty points to their thirty. With Canterbury and London Scottish going well in their matches, Richmond's chances of promotion were now beginning to look a bit thin.

But the club rallied and saw off Old Albanians 31-13 at home after which another day at The Athletic Ground meant that Haywards Heath travelled back to Sussex having been beaten 12-31. At Silver Leys, Bishop's Stortford conceded 8-29 and then we ran riot, thumping Tabard 99-0 at home.

A relief from the hard grind of the league gave Richmond the chance to host Purley John Fisher in the Surrey Cup Semi-final and that resulted in a very comprehensive win, 76-5. Following that game, back to the league and, in a complete downpour at Haywards Heath after a fairly even first half, we came away with 37 points under our belt to their 10.

The beginning of April took us to Sutton & Epsom's ground (a soggy one) to play Guildford & Godalming in the Final of the Surrey Cup and, in heavy rain, Richmond controlled the game and, yet again, took the silverware for the fifth time in six years, by 37 points to 13.

So then to the return fixture with London Scottish as the home side with so much depending on the result with a play-off for the winners to enter National League 3 South. A tough game was in prospect, especially after the trauma of the first game with our co-tenants but, on the day, Richmond were clearly in the ascendancy and ran out winners by 44 to 20, including two over 70 yard runs for tries after interceptions.

The last league game, a home fixture against Old Colfeians on a delightful Spring day, literally put spring into Richmond's feet and, although there was a brave effort by the opposition forwards, they could not avert a 97-5 drubbing. Richmond ended the season in second place in London 1.

A week later we were drawn at home in a play-off for promotion to National League 3 South against Clifton, second-placed in Southwest I. No tries were scored and our Avon opponents notched three drop goals and a penalty goal to our solitary penalty. So a season of high hopes ended with disappointment and meanwhile we remain in London 1.

The leading players supporting the Captain were Jo Ajuwa, Rupert Allhusen, Stuart Ault, Stewart Barlow, Matt Brown, David Connellan, Steve Dixon, Richard Emmerson, Ross Evans, Jono Farmer, Juliano Fiori, Joe Goatley, Owen Gregory, Matt Hart, Arthur Irving, John Lake, Tom Leigh, Alex Maclennan, Luke Mann, Cathal Murphy, Neil Piggot, Andy Saunders, Bob Skinstad, Chris Tennuci, Tristan Wesley, James Whitfield, Paul Wilson. Dan Taberner was injured in January for the remainder of the season and Matt Hart eased into the position as replacement captain with commendable ability. Chris Tennuci ended up as the league's top try scorer on 24 having overhauled James Whitfield, at hooker, in the final games. 'Whitty' ended up with 18, which said much for the dominance of the pack during the season.

Barbarian caps were awarded to Bob Skinstad bringing more honours to the Club but, on a very sad note, the year saw the passing of Ray Jenks who had served with distinction over many years as 300 Club Organiser and the impeccable administrator of our international tickets.

Chapter Six

The Heavies

This 'veteran' section of the club evolved from the old Extra A XV and such has been its successes - many seasons' records show no losses at all - both in this country and around the globe, that the very name has evoked envy of its existence. In fact, many similar teams in other clubs have been started because of the ethos surrounding the Heavies.

How did it begin? At the end of the 1960s, Murray Judd and Ernie Preece felt that, rather than lose players (elderly gentlemen) who could train only infrequently, they should become the basis of the Extra A. These players would be bolstered by youngsters who could benefit from the "flair, excitement, expertise, savoir-faire and poise of their mentors".

The idea gained a consensus of agreement but, strangely, it was five years before the annual Richmond Record made mention of the XV under its sobriquet with Ernie Preece as Captain - and a further five years before 'Extra A' disappeared from the fixture card and was replaced by the Heavies.

A synopsis of their raison d'Ître (apart from Murray and Ernie's conception) was that they should be composed mainly of ex 1st XV players, with the task of bringing on younger players and that the season should not start before pitches had softened and should finish when they began to harden in the spring or certainly by Easter (whichever was earlier!)

In the mid '80s it became the tradition that the new skipper was elected by ex-skippers who had played in the previous season. This took the form of a lunchtime get-together at Simpson's - discussions rarely started before the port, which flowed feely, and were known to go on well into the evening.

The rules for team selection were not too arduous but two spring to mind viz., a fine of a jug of gin and tonic if aspirants were spotted out training and a similar penalty for scoring a hat-trick. Schooners of sherry were de rigueur in the early days, frequently followed by a compulsory snifter on the field of play immediately prior to kick-off, or alternatively, an 'invigorator' at half time.

Such is the Heavies spirit on the field that many distinguished Internationals have striven to wear the jersey. In particular, the following names spring to mind - Terry Brooke, Tony Bucknall, Jeremy Janion, Tony Neary, Nick Preston, Chris Ralston, South Africans Tommy Bedford, Keith Oxlee and Harry Roberts, All Black Scott Cartwright and Wallaby Tommy

Lawton.

Off the field, members have spawned the Richmond Heavies' Golf Club and the Richmond Heavies Founders' Dinner - both of which have and continue to make a substantial financial contribution to the main club, the latter being greatly assisted by the persuasive powers of Chris Mills - the Heavy auctioneer. The Richmond Heavies Simpson's Luncheon Club, the Richmond Heavies Claret Club and the Richmond Heavies Dog Club (so called because the annual lunch in its early years, held to formulate investment strategy for the year ahead, took place between Christmas and New Year resulting in all members inevitably being in the Dog House!) have tended to drink any excess funds but are none the less representative of the Heavies' ethos for all that.

It has to be recorded that, on a very enterprising note, the Heavies in the 1980s clubbed together to buy a second-hand London Transport double-decker bus for transportation to away matches.

The vehicle was re-designed to incorporate an adequately stocked bar on the upper deck and was used for an away tour to the West Country but, well short of Exeter, things fell apart. The lively passengers hitched a lift from a passing empty coach on the M5 and, thanks to two stalwarts, the bus eventually reached Plymouth. However, subsequent investigations showed the damage to be beyond the means of the pockets of even these affluent gentlemen and that adventure perished.

Touring has always been a way of life for the Heavies and, in addition to playing when supporting 1st XV tours to South Africa (1976), the Far East (1978) and the United States (1980), these intrepid men have organised many of their own travels. Early destinations encompassed the Cayman Islands with Robin Robins (in conjunction with the Public School Wanderers) in charge in 1976 - which also included stop-offs in Freeport (Bahamas) and Miami, South Africa in 1979 under David Buchanan (ably assisted by 'Spike' Espey) and the French Caribbean in 1981 with Roddy Adams as leader where matches were played in Guadaloupe, Martinique and St Lucia.

In 1984, South Africa was again visited under David Chisnall with three wins out of four against the Wanderers in Johannesburg, Villagers and Bays Ba-Bas in Cape Town and Collegians in Durban. France followed under Steve Faktor and then it was Barbados with Terry O'Hanlon in May 1988.

Argentina was visited in 1991 with Ian Botes as skipper and Wim Bushell took the Heavies to Baltimore in the USA in 1993, playing three and winning three.

"Mod" Oliviera ran the show in 1995 in San Francisco where the side won two matches but lost in the final of the Golden Gate Vets' Tournament. The

United States was proving popular because in 1997, Richard Holman led a side to Austin, Texas with a 100% success record which he matched the following year in Zimbabwe. Mickey Conner was next to take the helm and he returned to Barbados in 1999 - two played, two won. The next year, the commitment to touring was undiminished but, while the Cuba National XV proved too strong, Ali Law's pride was later salvaged in Montego Bay, Jamaica.

Before he regrettably emigrated to Australia, Tim Griffin, the affable Welshman, led the side to Italy in 2001 where they entered the Treviso Vets (old timers not animal practitioners) Tournament and came away with the trophy.

In 2002/3, fourteen matches were played but two were lost-ending a two year unbeaten run, but a year later, in our first foray in the Surrey Veterans League, we claimed the championship by not losing (19 matches). This trophy was retained in the following year, during which the Japanese Osaka Vets presented the Club with a Samurai Helmet trophy.

The Heavies have also made their mark in France, Ireland and Scotland over the years.

That sums up the travelling prowess of the ancient stars with apologies for any omissions but it should be recorded that, in an international context, the Heavies were undefeated in the 1985 Golden Oldies Rugby Festival held at venues around London (including The Athletic Ground) fielding both over 35s and over 40s teams. This featured over 7,000 aged bodies from every continent and involved matches of three twenty minute periods with no tackling of septuagenarians and over.

In the years since the Heavies were formed, the Captains have been:

1971 - Ernie Preece
1972 - Tim Jacques
1973 - Ian Botes
1974 - Bob Blaney
1975 - Dave (Tripper) Allen
1976 - Robin Robins
1977 - Mike Morgan
1978 - David Buchanan
1979 - Phil (Filthy) Reid
1980 - Tony Stansfield
1981 - Steve (Heavy) James
1982 - Tony Bucknall
1983 - Gareth Thomas

1984 - David Chisnall
1985 - Ian (Wang) Diery
1986 - Steve Faktor
1987 - Terry O'Hanlon
1988 - Robert Brooks
1989 - Ray Edwards
1990 - Martin Slagter
1991 - Ian Ray
1992 - John (Sid) Wright
1993 - Wim Bushell
1994 - Brian Hester
1995 - Michael (Mod) Oliveira
1996 - Michael Hess
1997 - Richard Holman
1998 - Mickey Conner
1999 - Alastair Law
2000 - Tim Griffin
2001 - David Chisnall - for the second (and last?) time
2002 - Budge Prichenfried
2003 - Dougal Hawkes
2004 - Philip Williams
2005 - Rob Sterry
2006 - John Fenton

Finally, it should be pointed out that the Heavies have maintained their amateur status - in spite of many tempting offers.

Chapter Seven

Sevens Achievements

Although The Middlesex Sevens were started in 1926, Richmond achieved only moderate success in getting to the final of the competition for many years before our 'golden era' began in 1967. 1934 was the very first finals year when, after extra time, the Barbarians beat us 6-3. During the war years (when the tournament was held at The Athletic Ground) Richmond, playing as Richmond Wanderers, reached the final in 1940, losing 0-18 to Metropolitan Police.

Seven years later, back at Twickenham, we lost 6-12 to Rosslyn Park butthen, in 1951, Richmond II became the only second seven in the history of the short game ever to win the trophy, beating Wasps 13-10.

Two years later, in 1953, Richmond beat London Welsh 10-3 and in 1955 we won the trophy again, beating St Luke's College, Exeter, 5-0. However, it was not until 1967 that we next appeared in the final, losing 11-14 to Harlequins. The team on that occasion comprised Brian Stoneman (Capt.), Howard Waller, Jim Browntree, Ian Moffat, Tommy Bedford, Ernie Preece and Gavin Cormack. Our route to the final had recorded wins over Wasps 13-5, Moseley II 13-11 and Loughborough Colleges 16-5.

The following year Richmond I beat Richmond II 16-3, Blackheath 13-8 and Saracens 21-5, before losing in the final to London Welsh 3-16. The seven that year included Gavin Cormack (Capt.), Alan Blake, Howard Waller, Robin Whitcomb, Nigel Wilson, Ernie Preece and Bill Hadman.

During the years noted above Richmond had played preliminaries at various London venues and, in latter years, traditionally at Old Paulines, where, even though though fielding good sides, we often seemed to fall at the final hurdle (usually v Rosslyn Park). The Richmond Secretary, sensing the standard was not so good at Sunbury, appealed to Middlesex C.R.F.U to switch our early matches there. It did the trick because, between 1974 and 1983, Richmond achieved seven finals at Twickenham.

The 1974 final against London Welsh was a victory for Richmond by 34-16, and was the highest winning margin in the competition up to then and, as Richmond II also got to the semi-final, it was nearly a one club issue. After this success, the organisers made sure that, if two sevens of the same club reached the final stages at Twickenham, they would be placed in the same half of the draw. The 1974 win was achieved with victories over Upper Clapton 21-8, London Scottish 22-0 and North of Ireland 22-10, with a seven of Nigel Wilson (Capt.), Stuart Maxwell, Neil Boult, Pat Lavery, Tony Bucknall, Peter Hearn and Bill Hadman.

Richmond were at it again in the 1975 Jubilee Sevens when, under Pat Lavery's captaincy, supported by Stuart Maxwell, Neil Boult, Terry O'Hanlon, Bill Hadman, Peter Hearn and Tony Bucknall, wins over Esher 24-0, Old Emanuel 24-0 and Blackheath 18-10 produced a final against Loughborough Colleges which we won 24-8. The referee for that game was David Spyer, who has produced the bulk of these records for us. Loughborough Colleges included Colin Lambert, Ian Ray and Nigel Gillingham - all of whom were later to join Richmond and play for us with distinction.

We missed out in 1976 but, in 1977, victories over Blackheath 36-6, Leicester 34-0 and London Welsh 22-12 ensured a final against Gosforth, whom we beat 26-16, with a seven led by Roger Shackleton (sub Alan Mansfield), with the other players being Jeremy Janion, Terry O'Hanlon, Alan Mort, Neil Dobson, Neil Vinter and Charlie Yeomans.

Another win in the 1979 final over our co-tenants London Scottish 24-10, after victories over London Welsh 16-10 and Harlequins 18-6, was achieved by Terry O'Hanlon (Capt.), Nick Preston, Roger Shackleton, Ian Ray, Nick Mallett (later on in the 1990s to become South Africa's manager), Phil Williams and Rick Pearson.

We enjoyed yet another back-to-back with a victory in 1980, when the seven was again under the captaincy of Terry O'Hanlon, the other six being Colin Lambert, Ian Ray, Nick Preston, Neil Dobson, Neil Vinter and Charlie Yeomans. We saw off Borough Road College 18-4, London Welsh 28-4 and Wasps 20-18 before beating Rosslyn Park 34-18 in the final.

A blank year in 1981 but wins in 1982 over Harlequins II 20-10, London Welsh 18-6 and Harlequins I 12-6 saw us reach the final only to go under to Stewarts Meville FP by 12-34 with a seven consisting of Neil Vinter (Capt.), Nick Preston, Martin Humberstone, Ian Ray, Richard Mayle, John Fenton and Barry Crawshaw.

However, triumph was in the air again in 1983 when we beat London Welsh 20-13 after wins over Exeter University 16-0, London Scottish 24-10 and Rosslyn Park 8-4, having been led by Nick Preston, supported by Jim Dyston, Ian Ray, Terry O'Hanlon, Phil Williams, John Fenton and Barry Crawshaw.

The golden period was over with no further finals, although in 1993, having lost in the first round 12-19 to Northampton, Richmond played and beat Blackheath 14-7, Reading 26-14 and Basingstoke 36-7 to win the recently-inaugurated Plate competition with a squad under Mark Roper, who led Mark Venner, Eddie Saunders, Mike Hutton, John Makin, Douggie Elliot, Paul Greenwood, Ian Grisewood and David Hawkes.

We might have got there again in the Plate of 1999, having just lost to Gloucester 12-14 only to draw 21-21 with Harlow although, according to the scoreboard we were clearly ahead at the time - a fact corroborated by the referee. Our protests to Middlesex C.R.F.U officials fell on deaf ears and, because of torrential rain, no extra time could be played. Officialdom directed that the result should be decided on the toss of a coin and we lost. Further protests were ignored so Harlow were unfairly declared the winners. In fact, the final was never played because of the conditions.

It is worth noting that, in all the years above, most club sevens teams consisted entirely of 1st XV players whereas Richmond used chaps who excelled at the "short game", from whichever of our XVs. On a more recent note, Richmond "ran away" with the Middlesex County Bowl in 2002 with a massive 64-0 victory over Ealing.

Locally, the other main tournament in which Richmond featured was the Surrey County Sevens but only twice did the club reach the final, played at London Irish. The first year of these was, appropriately, in our centenary year - 1961. The squad that year comprised Mike Pope, Roger Segal, Ted Wates, Paul Charteris, Brian Zylstra, Greville Edgecombe (later known as "Low Level Greville" because of his exploits in Army aircraft), Bill Munks and Martin Ball. In the course of their run they beat Old Walcountians 13-0, Old Croydonians 18-0, KCS Old Boys 10-3 and Rosslyn Park 16-0 before taking the winner's rostrum with victory over Voyagers but, surprisingly, neither the local press nor Surrey records give the score in the final.

Our last appearance in the Surrey final until 2002 was in 1966 when we were subdued by the Harlequins to the tune of 0-26. On the way to that game we had beaten Raynes Park 6-0 and London Irish 10-0 with the players involved being Brian Dykes, Mike Pope, Tony Boyd-Smith, Ted Wates, Ian Palmer-Lewis, Simon Jones, John (The Judge) Aylwin, Peter Eastwood and David Kellar. The achievement in reaching the Final in 2002 was meritorious because it was the day we won the Middlesex Bowl Sevens - but two competitions in one day was too much and we went down 14-42 to Old Guildfordians.

The other major Sevens in which Richmond played were those at Galashiels and at Melrose (which, in 1884, was the forerunner of all other sevens) and where the club committee traditionally invited the winners of the previous year's Middlesex Sevens.

Our first appearance at the Greenyards at Melrose was in 1975 when we fielded the following players - Tony Bucknall, Neil Boult, Bill Hadman, Peter Hearn, Pat Lavery, Stuart Maxwell and Nigel Wilson - (the 1974 winning Middlesex Seven) who overcame Boroughmuir 14-10 after extra time before giving best to our hosts Melrose (tournament winners) 4-10. Back in 1967 for another taste of the splendid Borders hospitality, we suffered an ignominious defeat in the first round when we lost 12-16 to Gala after leading 10-nil, a result not appreciated by the home crowd who expected guest sides to progress, not go down to their local arch rivals. On this occasion the seven were John Deller, Peter Harding, Peter Hearn, Pat Lavery, Alan Mort, Phil Williams and Nigel Wilson.

With a squad of Steve Curran, Neil Dobson, John Gill (who replaced Lavery in the semi final), Pat Lavery, Terry O'Hanlon, Ian Ray, Phil Williams and Nigel Wilson, Richmond had better success in 1978 when we got to the semi-final after disposing of Edinburgh Academicals 14-4 and Langholm 14-0, before capitulating 6-26 to Kelso.

In 1980 there was a clear victory against Hawick 20-6 but, in the second round and after leading 10-0, West of Scotland just pipped us 12-10 when our squad included Neil Dobson, Graham Gilbert, Terry O'Hanlon, Rick Pearson, Ian Ray, Neil Vinter and Richard Vyvyan.

Back in 1981 at the Greenyards, our previous year's opponents, Hawick earned revenge against Richmond's seven of Mike Dick, Neil Dobson, Graham Gilbert, Colin Lambert, Chris Pritchard, Neil Vinter and Phil Williams and outclassed us to the tune of 22-8.

In 1983 we had our best tournament at Melrose in their Centenary Sevens. Keith Bassom, Barry Crawshaw, John Fenton, Terry O'Hanlon, Nick Preston, Ian Ray and Neil Vinter beat West of Scotland 26-12, Langholm 22-12, and Jedforest 24-6 before losing 6-30 in the semi-final to the eventual winners, French Barbarians, a team which included Serge Blanco.

The following year, our last at Melrose, gave us an opening victory of 14-8 over Melrose with a team comprising Micky Conner, Barry Crawshaw, Jim Dyson, John Fenton, Budge Priechenfield, Mark Preston and Ian Ray before Watsonians ran out easy victors against us 26-4.

A week earlier it had been our privilege to be invited as guests to the Gala Centenary Sevens and Micky Conner, Barry Crawshaw, Jim Dyson, John Fenton, Julian Lamb, Budge Priechenfield and Ian Ray were in excellent form, winning the trophy in the final in a nail-biting finish over Jedforest 22-20. In earlier rounds we had coasted against Langholm 22-10, Kelso 12-0 and Gala 22-6.

To defend our Gala Cup in 1985, Rick Crawford, John Fenton, Ricky Forde, Dave Guyatt, Martin Humberstone, Matt Jewers, Sean Kelly, Budge Priechenfield, Ian Ray and Charlie Vyvyan took the field at Netherdale, Galashiels, but, after a win over our hosts Gala 18-14, we lost surprisingly 10-14 to Ayr.

It was not to happen for us at Gala in 1988 when Boroughmuir scored 26 points to our 12 in the first round and Matt Brown, John Cullen, Jim Dyson, John Heaton, Nick Preston, Derek Rimmer and Dave Wilson went away empty-handed.

Mention should be made also of a tournament held in Sarlat in the Dordogne in 1977 when a French businessman impressed by the Middlesex Sevens set up an international competition hoping to inaugurate an on-going competition of the same nature. Richmond were asked to represent England, London Irish to represent Ireland, London Scottish to represent Scotland (strangely they declined and Heriots F.P stood in for them) and London Welsh to represent Wales against twelve French Clubs.

The British clubs were flown from Gatwick to Limoges in a private jet and then on by private train to Sarlat. French TV screened all the games but, unfortunately, hardly anybody turned up to watch the matches and the initiative was abandoned.

However, Richmond acquitted themselves well after a shaky first half, defeating London Welsh comprehensively in the final. Roger Shackleton skippered the squad, which consisted of Dave Rollit, Terry (compulsory Pernod for breakfast!) O'Hanlon, Charlie Yeomans, Ian Ray, Adrian Barnes, Rick Pearson, Neil Vinter and Phil Williams.

So ends the account of the major sevens tournaments, but mention should be made of all the players over the years who have represented the club in the following competitions for supporters of the short game - Berkshire, Chiltern, Esher Floodlit, Haig International at Murrayfield in 1982, Halifax London Festival in 1981, Loughborough Colleges, North Kent, Oxfordshire, Rosslyn Park Floodlit, Sevenoaks, Sussex, Worthing and Wrexham.

In the New Millennium, the Club has re-ignited its sevens commitment. We now compete in most major competitions and have won the Middlesex Bowl (twice) and Henley, and have been runners-up in the Rosslyn Park Floodlit Sevens.

Chapter Eight

Tours History

In 1963 Richmond embarked on the club's second major tour abroad. After this and over a period of thirty years, the club was to become famed as the one which toured the most (including, it is believed, overseas clubs), taking in all five continents and virtually circumnavigating the globe.

The 1963 tour took in Kenya following an earlier one to that country in 1951 when we established reciprocal terms with the Nondescripts Club in Nairobi. Tour manager was Charlie Hopwood who had captained Richmond, Middlesex, Barbarians and was an ex England trialist, together with being a former Cambridge University representative on the R.F.U., and who had managed combined Oxford/Cambridge tours to Argentina in 1948, South Africa and Kenya in 1951.

Matches were played with the following results:

West Kenya	Eldoret	Won 26-6
Uganda	Nakuru	Won 37-3
Kitale and District	Kitale	Won 16-5
Kenya Central Province	Ngong Road, Nairobi	Won 16-0
Kenya Regiment	Ngong Road, Nairobi	Won 21-0
NAC(Invitation XV)	Nakuru	Won 19-6
Coast Province	Mombassa	Won 14-3
East Africa	Ngong Road, Nairobi	Lost 8-11
Nondescripts	Parklands, Nairobi	Won 29-12

The players on the tour were Bobby Burns, Robin Butler, Paul Charteris, Peter Cheesman, Peter Cook, Graham Fox, David Froud, David (Dai) Hawkes, Tony Hole, Murray Judd, Eric Lipscombe, Bill Munks, Pat Orr, Ian Palmer-Lewis, Mike Pope, Ernie Preece, Steve Smith, Brian Stoneman, Peter Thorning, Tony Vyvyan and Geoffrey Windsor-Lewis.

New ground was broken in 1969 when the club chartered an aircraft to the U.S.A. with Saracens who stayed in New York and Washington, whereas Richmond was the first British club to go beyond those cities. The Tour Manager, John Riley, a sailor in Combined Ops during the Second World War who had played for Waterloo and Lancashire, led a team of Brian Stoneman, as Assistant Manager; Mike Campbell, as Tour Secretary and Tony Stansfield in charge of

Publicity and Advertising.

The playing side was led by Ernie Preece, the club captain, and included James Aarvold, David (Tripper) Allen, John (The Judge) Aylwin, Andrew Barker, John Baron, Peter Baron, John Bell, Alan Blake, Tony Bucknall, Geoff Clarke, Peter Cook, Alan Fleming, Jonathan Harvey, David (Dai) Hawkes, Peter Hearn, Mike Humphreys, Robin Joliffe, Pat Lavery, Brian (Benny) Lee, Andrew Peters, John Powell-Rees, Chris Ralston, Ben Russell, Anthony Sharp, John (Titch) Taylor, Chris Waterman, Nigel Wilson and Dean Wotherspoon.

The tour encompassed two matches in Chicago - v Mid West Rugby Union (won 9-3) and Chicago Lions (won 9-6) and the touring party then went on to play Atlanta RFC (won 30-8) before visiting Virginia, where we played Richmond RFC (won 27-3). On then to play Washington RFC (won 26-8), Baltimore RFC (won 9-6), before finishing up in New York where matches against Metropolitan N.Y.R.U XV and Westchester RC recorded a loss of 3-16 and a win of 14-0 respectively. This was an interesting tour because it took in the centennial anniversary of rugby union football in the USA.

No other tours were planned but the Secretary noticed that old playing members of rival London clubs always seemingly retired to areas in their own vicinity and regularly visited Public Schools to recruit players, whereas retired leading Richmond members went to live in counties far away and did no recruitment. So he suggested that to counteract this, given our success in overseas touring, we should embark on bi-annual tours so that Richmond could become known as the leading club at this enterprise and would therefore encourage players to join us.

The committee agreed on the proviso that no expense should be borne by the club and this was agreed. Consequently, future travels abroad would be funded by direct liaison with the airways (i.e. no tour operators), money would be raised by a contribution from each tourist who also had to sell advertising space for the brochure and the remainder would be raised by sponsored walks (e.g. The London Bridges walk starting at Tower, going on to Chelsea and back to Tower, some 13½ miles), discos and swipecards.

To make the start on this project more feasible, it was decided to visit East Africa again in 1972. It had an auspicious start on East African Airways because by Frankfurt we had drunk the plane dry - refuelling needed! This was provided and, on landing at Entebbe in Uganda, a certain leading national rugby correspondent had to be taken into the airport building on a stretcher! He recovered.

The tour started at Kampala in Uganda and, because of the unrest that commenced a few weeks after our departure, we were, it is believed, the last club side to visit that country, Managed by Alan Skeats, who was supported by

Murray Judd (President), and Colin Holman (coach) the playing side was captained by Steve James.

A small crisis arose at the first match v Uganda, described by leading journalist Basil Easterbrook in later years "Alan Skeats has managed more than one of the long range tours and must qualify as one of the very few men to set aside a decision by Idi Amin and get away with it. The President announced his intention of attending the game and would graciously allow himself to be presented to the English party. After waiting in line for twenty minutes Skeats told the local officials he intended to start the game. There were shocked expressions and entreaties to wait for the dictator. After another five minutes failed to produce any sign of Amin, Mr Skeats said 'either we start the match now or it will not take place'. His ultimatum worked and, in the event, Amin never arrived. He had gone to another event elsewhere in the country. Needless to say, Richmond received neither explanation or apology. If Richmond ever go back that way they do not anticipate such a problem rising again." Richmond won the game 55-12.

By road then to Nakuru where West Kenya were beaten 69-4, before the Equator was crossed en route to Nairobi where, at Ngong Road, Kenya failed to score against Richmond's 28 points. The same ground was used the next day when we beat Scorpions 28-18.   Two days later, after a flight over Kilimanjaro, Richmond were, it is thought, the first and last 'club' side ever to play in Tanzania and met the national side in Dar-es-Salaam, where another victory was recorded to the tune of 56-0. Back to Nairobi where the game against our affiliated club Nondescripts resulted in a 34-9 win at Parklands, and the final match was versus a Combined East Africa XV at Ngong Road where a hundred per cent tour victory record was chalked up, the result being 19-9 in Richmond's favour.

Under Steve James, the players were James Aarvold, Mark Brickell, Tony Bucknall, Bill Campbell, John Deller, Bill Hadman, Peter Hearn, Mike Humphreys, Tony Kitchin, Pat Lavery, Pat Liddiard, Humfrey Malins (currently MP for Woking), Mike Marshall, John Martin, Leigh Merrick, Michael Moor, Peter Moore, Adrian Neale, Maurice Ridley, Mike Sale, Rod Scholes, Brian Slatter, Brian Strong and Nigel Wilson.

It was planned to tour Canada in 1974 but, unfortunately, relations between ourselves and officials on the other side of the pond broke down so it was not until 1976 that Richmond set out, again breaking new trails.

This time it was to South Africa (where in the past we had recruited such rugby names as Roy Allaway (our skipper in 1956), Tommy Bedford, Derek van den Berg, Jon Fellowes-Smith, Chick Henderson (who, alas, passed on in November 2006, just as this history was going to press), Theo Lombard, Richard

Steyn, Alistair Thom, Hugo and Piet Van Zyl) with a finish up in Rhodesia - again it is believed that Richmond were the first club to tour there.

The President, John Riley, toured in full regalia and the Tour Manager was Alan Skeats with Roger Shackleton leading the on the field party. Players selected for the tour were Colin Ashby, Adrian Barnes, Mark Brickell, Jonathan Dickins, Willie Dickinson, Gary Greenwood, Peter Harding, Peter Hearn, Michael Hess, Mike Humphreys, Steve James, Pat Lavery, Bob McGrath, Alan Mort, Terry O'Hanlon, Rick Pearson, Peter Philp, Ian Ray, Neil Vinter, David Whibley and Phil Williams.

The opening venue was Durban with a fixture against Natal University which we lost 10-22, followed by a combi ride to the Umfolozi River where everybody enjoyed a braai with our hosts from Zululand. They took us to the Hluhluwe Game Park where entertainment was provided with Zulu singing and dancing, to which Richmond replied with their own brand of "singing" and the presentation of a club tie and tour key ring to their leader. After observing the wild life, the team moved on to Empangeni where the second match was played in front of local Senator, Mr Botha. The outcome was in favour of the home side who won 15-11.

Then back to Durban, where the match against Richmond's affiliated club, Collegians, was played as a curtain-raiser to the Springbok v All Blacks Test Match at Kings Park, with the South Africa XV including Derek van den Berg, as mentioned earlier. The humidity affected us but we gave a spirited performance and lost 7-21. Four days later we were still trying to become acclimatised to the High Veldt after a visit to the Cullinan Diamond Mine organised by former Richmond player and member of staff, Howard Rigg. Facing high altitude conditions after playing on the coast meant that Pretoria Harlequins were able to beat us thoroughly 40-13.

Goodbye to the hospitality of South Africa and on to Salisbury, Rhodesia where our hosts treated us to two days at Victoria Falls before we faced the Goshawks (the local equivalent of the Barbarians) in front of the august presence of the then Prime Minister, Ian Smith, who insisted on meeting the party. The tour finished on a high note with a 21-20 victory, thanks to the boot of David Whibley.

So where did Richmond go next? It proved to be the Far East in 1978 when tour management was in the hands of Steve James with his assistant Mike Humphreys. The starting point was in Hong Kong where we were billeted in an Army barracks in Kowloon, sharing with a detachment of Gurkhas.

As in South Africa two years earlier, a strong contingent of Heavies supported the tour and showed their prowess on the pitch whilst captain Roger Shackleton led the senior side into the first game v Combined Services which resulted in a victory. A second game in the city produced a 26-17 score in our favour against the Hong Kong Chairman's XV. A heart fluttering flight on Philippine Airlines took the party to Manila where we arrived safely. Stan (The Shout) Burling as Baggage Man, having been warned by the Management of the strict customs laws in the islands, successfully managed to "smuggle" his "contraband" anti-mosquito and salt tablets past the watchful officials. Success went to his head, as he carried through the same operation on leaving the country.

For the first game (after the cows and their droppings had been cleared off the pitch) the outcome against Manila Nomads was a win by 56 points to nil. The fourth fixture of the tour featured a game at Clark Air Base against the U.S Air Force Red Barons where Richmond proceeded to a 60 points to 4 victory.

After shooting the rapids on the Pagsanjan River, the party proceeded to Singapore where Stan Burling's heavy night noises were noted again (as they had been originally in South Africa) and we were due for a late afternoon kick-off against New Zealand Forces S.E Asia. The match, which we won, was played in such humidity that all the players were stretched out on the dressing room floor for at least one and a half hours after the final whistle.

The second match in the city was played at the home of Singapore C.C at the Padang where, in 1945, the surrender of the Japanese was accepted. The result was in our favour over Singapore C.C President's XV.

A flight to Kuala Lumpur brought us to a match on that city's Padang against Selangor State R.U Invitation XV which went in Richmond's favour. Away from the intense humidity there to the "coolness" of Penang Island from where we ferried across to the mainland to meet Australian Forces North XV at Butterworth resulting in another win for us.

The hard slog over, half the party be-sported themselves for four days in the pool at the Penang Hotel whilst the more adventurous sampled the delights of Bangkok before returning to the island for the flight home.

The players who represented us were Jeff Bannister, Adrian Barnes, Tony Bucknall, Steve Curran, Jonathan Dickins, Willie Dickinson, Gary Greenwood, Ken Hall, Michael Hess, Brian Hester, Paul Morris, Alan Mort, Rick Naish, Terry O'Hanlon, Nick Preston, Chris Pritchard, Chris Rose, Chris Sharpe, Jerry Smith, Neil Vinter, David Whibley and Paul Williams.

In 1981 positions changed - Mike Humphreys assumed tour Managership and Steve James became his deputy and another British first was achieved when Richmond visited Hawaii as part of the Pacific Tour. The bearded Michael Hess captained the side which included Jeff Bannister, Adrian Barnes, Vinny Codrington, Mike Dick, Steve Faktor, Terry Fearn, Peter Gibson, Peter Harding, Brian Hester, Alan Mort, Rick Pearson, Nick Preston, Chris Ralston, Ian Ray,

RICHMOND FOOTBALL CLUB

Our History in Pictures
Section Two

1990-2006 - a period in which the club rose to its highest-ever standing in the game by finishing 5th in the Premiership - and sank to its lowest point by being relegated to Herts/Middlesex I.

This record relegation (by nine divisions) was quickly followed by a national record run of 84 consecutive league victories.

Who better to introduce this section than current Club Captain and RFCL Director, Andy Cuthbert, whose playing career spanned this whole period and was rewarded by selection for the Barbarians.

Richmond FC 1st XV 1991-2

Back Row: J.G. De L. Willis, H.M. Lamb, D. Sole, C. Lloyd, D.S. Elliott, M.J. Hutton, P.M.Williams

Centre Row: D. Hilliard (Coach), M.W. Hudson, W.A. Deeley, A. McKay, J. Foster, R.S. Banks, T.J. Benson, D. Cooper, J.E. Lewis, M.J.H. Brown, J.M. Satterley, A.V.H. Skeats (Tough Judge)

Front Row: Miss N. Jones (Physio), J.J. Hoad, D. Goodwin, P.J. Quinnen (Secretary), K.G. Boroevich (Captain), G.M. de P. Tardif (President), R.A. Ryden, S.R.A. Miller, M. Livesey

Ball Boys: R. Nothers, M. Owen, A. Walker-Robson

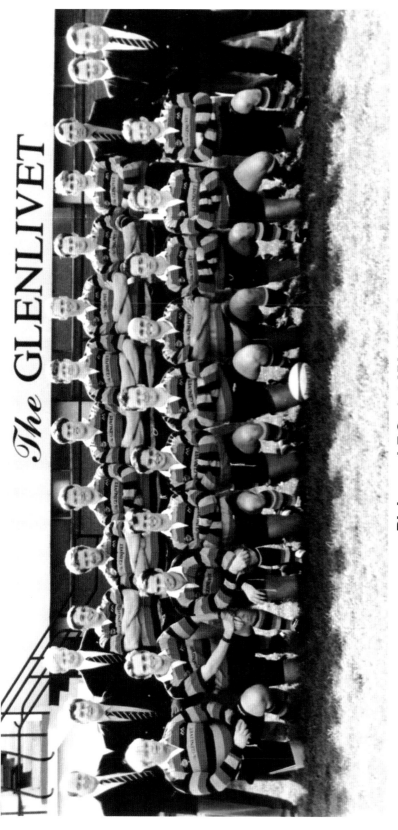

The GLENLIVET

Richmond F.C. 1st XV 1995-6

D. Taylor (Coach), D. Buchanan (President), C. Palmer, A. Cuthbert, M. Yeldham, J. Foster, M. Fitzgerald, P. Carr, G. Sage, L. Jones, R. Gavin, M. Hess (Chairman), J. Kingston (Head Coach), N. Griffiths (Manager)

D. Goodwin, J. Kottler, B. Short, A. Boyd, D. Elliott, M. Hutton (Captain), P. Della-Savina, D. Luger, J. Gregory, J. Clarke

Professional Players

There are some of the great players who graced the club during the professional era - on and off the field of play.

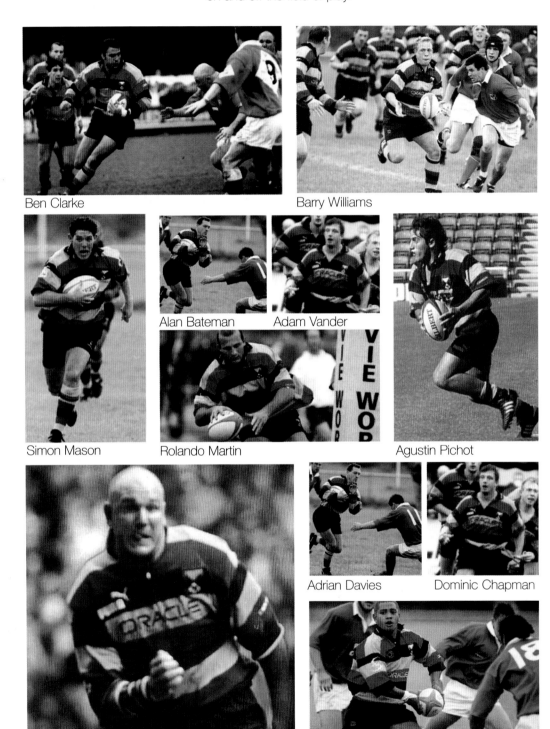

Ben Clarke

Barry Williams

Alan Bateman

Adam Vander

Simon Mason

Rolando Martin

Agustin Pichot

Adrian Davies

Dominic Chapman

Craig Quinnell

Earl Va'a

Richmond F.C. First XV 1997-8

Top: S. Brown, B. Leigh, A. Cuthbert, R. Hutton, B. Williams, R. Martin, J. Davies, D. Chapman, A. Pichot, A. Bateman

Middle: T. Exeter (Fitness Coach), M. Hutton, J. Foster, D. Crompton, C. Quinnell, R. West, C. Gillies, P. Carr, C. Palmer, M. Fitzgerald, D. McFarland, J. Kingston (Director of Rugby)

Bottom: R. Lowzoski, M. Deane, E. Va'a, A. Moore, M. Pini, A. Davies, B. Davies, B. Clarke (Captain), S. Mason, B. Harvey, A. Vander, J. Wright, S. Cottrell, M. Pearson (Physio)

Relaunch Day - October 1999. Lots of important people and some grown-ups release the balloons.

Management Committee 2003-4

P. Moore (Finance Director), H. Ives (Women's Chair), L. O'Keefe (Women's Club Captain), R. Humphrey (Richmond Players' Jobs Bureau), M. Anderson (Chairman of Minis), A. Maren (Head of Coaching)

D. Corben (Richmond Business Group), J. Gadsby Peet (Assistant Treasurer), A. Gordon (Secretary/General Manager), T. Hallett (Chairman), I. Botes (President), A. Cuthbert (Captain), A. Quigley (Chairman of Senior Playing), Not shown - Harry Hooper (Communications/Travel/Logistics)

Richmond's Minis

We could fill a whole book with the achievements of Richmond's Mini Rugby Section.
Here are just a few: -

In1998 the Richmond 300 Club contributed £4,000 to the inaugural Richmond Mini Tournament - an event which has gone from strength to strength since then. The cheque was presented by Ray Jenks - long time organiser of the 300 Club.

Mini action - Michael Simpson (U10 here) was selected for England U16 in 2005

The Mini formula - a careful balance between practice and competition.

Richmond's Minis

Under 10s - Winners, Gullivers National Tournament, Twickenham, 2000

Under 7s - Winners Chiltern Festival, 2004

Under 11 A - Nottingham, 2005

Under 11 B - Winners, Surrey County Festival, 2005

Richmond's Minis

Under 11s at Twickenham - May 2005

2006 - on Tour in Wales

Under 8s - Winners, Surrey A, 2005

End of term. The 2005-6 Under 12s display all their trophies at the end of their Mini careers.

Richmond 1993 U14 Tour to Wales

Standing: N. Litwinek, A.H. Stephenson, A.L. McGill, B.D. Hillman, E.G. Hallett, J.P. Allred, E.G. de Vroome, F.J. Frazer, A.J. Beattie, T.J. Cahill, A.P. Curry

Seated: W.N. Harris, J.P. Driscoll, A. MacDonald, C. Pataras, S. Buchanan (Captain), D. Taberner, N. Clisby, O.J. Quigley, O.M. Thomas

Richmond Colts Middlesex U19 7s Champions 1999-2000

N. Skinner, N. Davis, W. Beeley, N. Tillin, S. Codrington, J. Whelan, K. Bell (Coach)

O. Walbyoff, A. Ambrose (Captain), K. Rothwell, C. Hotchkiss

Richmond FC Colts Season 2000-1

Back: M. Banks (Coach), D. Armstrong, S. Mapanza, O. Saddler, N. Failes, C. Hotchkiss, R. Skinner (Coach), M. Knights (Coach)

Front: N. Skinner, T. Gerlach, M. Jones (Captain), I. Asl, N. Stein, S. Knights (Mascot)

NATIONAL CHAMPIONS

RICHMOND FOOTBALL CLUB Under 16s 2003/04

Coaches   Steve Conlon   Anthony Rands   Nick Jewell

(Manager & Hd Coach)
Mike Reilly   Phil Wade

Jack Franklin   Mikael Ahola   Jack Newbury   David North   Tom Loizides   Sam Paterson   Jack Rands
Conor Sullivan   Akin Williams   Baz Wakefield   Micky Freeman   Henry   Matt Conlon-Perry   Will Cusack
Montgomery-Smith

Michael Molony   Jake Haworth   Seb Jewell   Elliot Moger   Shane Feely
Matt Reilly   Tom Wade   Oli Grindrod (Capt)   Billy Keates

Winners of the 16@16 Competition. Lichfield 2004

Richmond Women's Section

Our Women's Section is a successful and vibrant part of the club where much has been achieved in a relatively short time -see Chapter 9

Richmond Women 1994-5

Alas, we have been unable to identify every member of this highly-successful group (League and Cup winners) Hopefully, missing names will identify themselves in time for the reprint of this bestselling history.

Back: Mark Francis, Jane Miles, ----- , Helen Flippance-Street, ----- , ----- , ----- , Kate Adams,Rochelle Martin, Els Vermeulen, Terri Siwek, Jenny Sutton, Kathy Jenn, Jenny Chambers, Pogo Paterson, Sarah 'Wurzel', Anna Richards, ----- , Carol Isherwood, Katie Munn, Karen Duckworth, ----- .

Middle: ----- , Katie Mullen, ----- , Andrea Williams, Sarah Wenn, ----- , Adrienne Tari, Mel Fogg, Sue Ellis, Debbie Francis, Dee Mills, Vicky Sheriff, Nicki Coffin, ----- , Gillian.

Front: ----- , ----- , Kath Vass, Sally Bryant, Andrea Rabin, Karen Findlay, Sue Dorrington, Sarah Escott, Suzanne Lambert, Helen Bullock, Eileen Cunningham, Janet 'Wigan' Livesey, ----- , Karen Penney, ----- , ----- .

Richmond F.C. Womens Section 1997-8

Back Row: Karen Findlay, Raeltine Shrieves, Victoria Wiseman, Sue Wachholz-Dorrington, Debbie Francis, Kathy Jenn, Maureen MacMahon, Jenny Sheerin, Terri Siwek, Jenny Sutton, Nicky Jupp, Nicky Coffin, Jo Poore, Cantel de Senna, Sophie Peterson, Miriam Williams

Middle Row: Sarah Rochester, Wendy Shaw, Karen Gilliard, Bridget Lavin, Lisa Bailey, Katie Mullen, Tamsin Reed, Venessa Young, Rebecca Tuck, Felicity Booth, Eryka Wessell, Jo Brownley, Helen Flippance, Venessa Gray

Front Row: Jen Dickson, Montse Martin, Sharon Whitehead, Jess Morris, Sharon Murphy, Claire Hoppe, Helen Ives, Lisa Cuss, Karen Campbell, Louise Anderson, Ann Bamford

Richmond Women - National Cup Winners 2005-6

The Gareth Savin Trust

The club has made a commitment to Gareth and the walk from Blackheath to Richmond, which commemorates the oldest club rugby fixture, has raised substantial funds for the Trust.

9th April 2005 - The beginning of a great day as the walkers leave Blackheath.

Lunch...

Gareth Savin

The walkers (Left to right). John Nicholls, Juliet Stephenson, Ian Botes, Ian Capon. Jules Boardman, David Corben, Juliet Stephenson, Ian and Heather Ray and, of course, Gareth.

The Heavies contribution to the club is immense. Here the elegantly-attired Heavies prepare to run in support of the Gavin Savin Trust. They all looked a little less elegant 4 miles later... (the dog was ok)

More Heavies Magic

Toad of Eff Hall - another substantial contribution to the culture and coffers of the club.

Moley (Kirwan)

Badger (Vallings)

Ratty (Morgan)

Stoatsey (Botesy)

Washerwoman (Blundell - Williams) and
Gaoler's Daughter (Edwards)

Bullocks (Robins)

Toady (Reid) and Prod (Blaney)

Special Day

22nd February 2004. We beat Sidcup 75-3 to clinch promotion to London Division 1. It is also the 75th consecutive league victory and, by the time this photograph was taken, the queue at the bar was already four deep - so these are genuine supporters indeed.

Back to the Future (October 2005)

Richmond and local friends and rivals, Barnes, join forces to commemorate the first match under the Football Association rules of 1863 which was played between the two clubs and featured in a Granada TV series presented by Melvyn (Lord) Bragg.

High Fashion at Richmond

Richmond has always been a well-dressed club and the club shop plays an important role as merchandise deals are an increasingly important source of revenue. Eden Park, Gilbert and Canterbury are three of our distinguished suppliers. Here's how we looked in the mid-1990s.

Inset: Vinny Codrington, Richmond's first Director of Rugby models an elegant waistcoat.

Richmond's touring tradition has been maintained throughout the club in the post-professional era. Here we show the 1st XV squad's successful tour to Canada in 2001. The squad toured South Africa in 2006.

The Long Road Back...

Here are just a few memories on the road from Herts/Middlesex I.

The Long Road Back (contd)

Richmond FC Development Squad 2003-4

Back: N. Nason, T. Gerlach, A. Haggart, J. Collingson, N. Gill, S. Hallett

Middle: R. Skinner (Coach), K. Bell (Coach), A. Culley, A. Walker, M. Drayson, D. Knight, B. Wassell, O. Cochrane, J. Gadsby Peet, M. Cooper, T. Shattock, E. Metcalfe, J. Manser (Manager)

Front: S. Barlow, B. Sullivan, K. Luckman (Captain), S. Clarke, N. Skinner, D. Rawlings

Richmond F.C. Saxons 2003-4

Back: R. Roberts, G. Neal, R. Parry, G. Smith, D. Hunt, H. Payne

Middle: B. Lewis, J Samuel, M. Hardaker, E. Horner, R. Cross, H. Stevenson, H.Williams, G. Baber, B. Gutteridge, H. Stevens
S. Buchanan, C. Adkins, D. Mannion, T. Barham

Front: H. Newton, R. Kennedy, James, A. Davey (Captain), R. Kenworthy, N. Thatcher, A. Johnson

Richmond F.C. Vikings 2003-4

Back: J. Pye, R. Kothakota, S. Lodder, J. Whitfield, T. Hood, J. Croker, V. Holden, M. Chicken

Middle: A. Quigley, J. Mulholland, M. Exworthy, D. James, O. Quigley, M. Hemmell, T. Sedgewick, T. Amako, L. Lonergan, Z. Higgins, J. Joyce, A. Leigh, L. Hughes

Front: M. Slattery, T. Price, O. Bishop, M. McSweeney (Captain), Y. Rahmanzadeh-asl, J. Samuel, M. Clifford, J. Peckitt

Richmond F.C. 1st XV 2003-4

Back: S. Lodder, M. Slattery, A. Bamford, M. McSweeney, H. Head, O. Bishop, T. Hood, T. Sedgewick

Middle: A. Hallett (Chairman), J. Evans (Manager), M. Cuthbert (Physio), A. Quigley (Chairman, Senior Playing), R. Humphrey (Players Bureau), M. Bolton, P. Enright, D. James, J. Whitfield, N. Piggot, M. Brown, L. Gunn, S. Dixon, R. Thomas, R. Evans, O. Quigley, N. Thatcher, S. Morrison, V. Holden, M. Clifford (Physio), M. Knights (Coach), I. Botes (President), A. Maren (Head Coach)

Front: T. Stokes, A. Maclernan, O. Gregory, R. Allhusen, A. Cuthbert (Captain), D. Taberner, S. Barlow, A. Greally, B. Leigh

Richmond F.C. 1st XV 2005-6

Back: R. Emmerson, S. Ault, S. Dixon, C. Murphy, J. Farmer, J. Fiori

Middle: D. Corben (Chairman), I. Taplin (Fitness), M. Knights (Coach), J. Joyce (Coach), D. Shaw, O. Gregory, J. Ajuwa, M. Brown, C. Tennuci, D. Connellan, A. Maren (Head Coach), A. Quigley (Chairman, Senior Playing), S. Morrison (Physio), A. Hallett (President)

Front: T. Leigh, J. Whitfield, R. Allhusen, D. Taberner (Captain), M. Hart, A. Maclennan, S. Barlow, M. Bolton

Chris Sharpe, Jerry Smith, Jim Thorn, Neil Vinter, David Whibley, Phil Williams, Dave Willis and Martin Wood and support was given by Brian (Belgrave Bullett) Kirwan on Press and PR (and Johnny Walker) and Tony Stansfield on Advertising.

The tour is best summed up by the following extract from Mike Humphreys' report in the Richmond Newsletter - "Forty six members were on tour and all but four of our "senior citizens" took the field at one time or another. Alan Skeats is worthy of special mention here as a result of his sound game as full back for the Heavies in San Francisco, coming close to a daring try in the second half. The 1st XV won all five games but not without considerable effort and, as it turned out, each game was harder than the last.

Our first fixture v New York Metropolitan resulted in a 36-12 win, admittedly against a side weakened by US National Trials, and New York was memorable for training sessions in Central Park and Chris Ralston being robbed. Members will remember Bill Hadman visiting New York from Nairobi where he now lives. He turned out for the Heavies against Old Blue Heavies, as did Harris Wainwright Jnr who was playing for us only two years before. A tough fixture on a very rough pitch and we did well to force a 15-15 draw."

Arriving in San Francisco " the tour was aghast that bars and restaurants closed at 2.00 am against virtually all night sessions in New York. However, we were relieved to discover that they opened again at 6.00 am! The match arranged for us here was against Davis City, about 70 miles inland towards Sacramento. The Heavies played first and were horrified by the age of the opposition - not a veterans side but Davis City 2nd XV. Legs ran out and we were well beaten. The 1st XV gained revenge with a score of 18-11 - we had done a good missionary job at Davis City who had not experienced rugby tourists before and it helped them not only in playing the game but in developing their attitudes towards it.

We departed for the jewel in the tour - Hawaii - it really is a long way from England and we were generally assumed to be Australians. That even includes Mike Dick! The rugby opposition was boosted by Aussies, New Zealanders and some swarthy Samoans but our lads were equal to the struggle and came out in front 19-11 against Hawaii Harlequins and 9-6 against an Hawaiian Invitation XV. The Hawaiians had expected to win as they had recently beaten Eastern Suburbs of Sydney. The Heavies also won well.

After a week in Hawaii, we went back to the mainland and Los Angeles where, the next day, the whole tour visited Disneyland and the revelation emerged that Robin Robins' mother had once been engaged to Walt Disney.

The final game was against Los Angeles RFC of whom six had played against Wales B three weeks before. Best pitch of the tour at California State

University against strong opposition and the final score was 12-9. The Heavies played their best tour match and beat Old Frothians."

Warm climes yet again when Richard (Roddy) Adams managed the tour to Fiji and Australia in 1983 supported by President Alan Skeats, Captain Mike Hess, baggage man Stan Burling (displaying the same nocturnal noises), and Graham Beaumont, the wandering referee. Quotations hereafter are taken from the pen of the manager commencing with "the horrendous 30 hour journey to Fiji with an enjoyable stopover in Vancouver. Excitement rose as the South Seas approached and then, first by windowless coach then by an old tub, veteran of the Dunkirk evacuation, we travelled to Beachcomber Island.

We won comfortably our opening match against Lautoka Police Club by 43-6 "(in spite of Graham Beaumont refereeing)", had the plane delayed 5 hours "travelled with former Richmond player David Moeller and were met at Sydney by Renny Cunnack" (1965 Vikings Captain) where we shared accommodation and training facilities with New Zealand Club Taranaki who we out-scrum-maged in the local park.

In normal circumstances, the Manly fixture would have been cancelled due to the incessant rain throughout our stay in Sydney. However they fixed us up on a half flooded park pitch where, despite plentiful possession, we lost 0-3.

In the game against Randwick, our star-studded opponents (a brace of Ellas, Poinderin etc) were 0-9 down at half-time. Thirty points on the second half rather flattered our hosts" but "Manly and Randwick are in fact the top two clubs in Sydney so we took no soft options with the fixtures". So 9-30 was not too bad.

"We coached to Canberra in the continuing rain" where "Ray Edwards' club, Norths, hosted us" and, at Rugby Park, we had a "10-6 victory against A.C.T Presidents XV also featuring a promising newcomer, David Campese. Original tour captain Chris Sharpe, Alf Shortland and Bill Reichwald, who were only able to join us after Sydney, played only 10 minutes before retiring. A.C.T later beat Argentine Pumas 35-9."

Sunshine at last when we hit Surfer's Paradise prior to a match against Queensland B (reinforced by four capped players) when "a half time deficit was turned into a stunning 27-19 victory" at Ballymore. Andrew James even kicked a goal from his own half - "Ballymore had not seen anything like it since Alan Old for England in 1975".

"It was good to have Alan Skeats on tour and our reputation was enhanced by his presence and the tour party, the club and I owe the lot to Mike Hess who took on the captaincy at short notice and made a major contribution to the success."

The touring party of the players comprised Mike Catt, Mickey Conner, Barry

Crawshaw, Ray Edwards, Trevor Evans, Steve Faktor, John Fenton, Dougie Goodwin, Andrew James, Chris Makaness, Robin Osborne, Simon Pennock, Nick Preston, Bill Reichwald, Chris Sharpe, Alf Shortland, Martin Slagter, Hugh Stevenson, Jim Thorn, Neil Vinter, Neil Whitehead, Lawrence Williams and Phil Williams.

In 1986 another debut - we are again believed to be the first British club to visit Paraguay and Brazil - and extracts from Tour Manager Roddy Adams report the effervescent spirit which pervades every Richmond tour. In a clean sweep of results, support was given by the tour management of John Wright (Assistant Tour Manager), Andy Hampel (Captain), John Cullen (Vice Captain), Brian Hester (Coach), Roger Hurst (Medical) and Alan Skeats (Immediate Past President).

On the field Richmond were represented by Steve Allum, Simon Attfield, Wim Bushell, Micky Conner, Martin Drane, Ray Edwards, Steve Faktor, John Fenton, Dougie Goodwin, Richard Holman, Mark James, Mel Jones, Dave Kenningham, Chris Mackaness, Jim McKenzie, Tim Martineau, Chris Mills, Mike Oliviera, Simon Pennick, Nick Preston, Mark Roper, Bruce Roxburgh, Martin Slagter, David Sole, Paul Southern, John Turner and Phil Williams, with Graham Beaumont instilling his refereeing expertise into bemused locals.

The extracts from the manager's report commence with "It is fitting that the club's 125th anniversary ended in style with one of the happiest major tours ever. While Alan Skeats and Phil Williams have done all the continents, it was good to see many new tourists. Strong playing opposition was not really expected but it was nevertheless disappointing how weak it was, as the results show. It is to the player's credit that they did not allow their attitude towards the matches and training to deteriorate. What they may lack in rugby skills, our hosts and opponents certainly made up for in kindness and hospitality. The Paraguayans show signs of improvement and, since they play Argentina regularly, it is hardly surprising."

At Asunción we recorded victories over The City XV 42-10 and the Paraguay National XV 48-7, after which an enjoyable stop was made at Iguaco waterfalls before proceeding to São Paulo where the facilities of the Athletic Ground were enjoyed and where " we entered four teams in a seven- a- side competition organised by the Brazilian R.U. Two of our sevens contested the final in the dark of a late evening, the result in consequence being still in dispute."

Our three main matches there resulted in wins over Medecina 104 -6 and S.P.A.C/ Alphaville 82-10 and finally Bardeirantes/São Paulo F.C 106-0. Roddy Adams continues "to finish a tour in an hotel on Copacabana Beach" (We were now in Rio de Janeiro) "is the stuff of Hollywood script writers and, in the suburb of Niteroi, we ran up 80 points to the home side's 15."

A five year break before Richmond ventured on a major tour again and, in

1991, it was South America again where, it is understood, we were the first British club side to visit Argentina. We arrived in Buenos Aires for a night's stop before flying on to San Juan in the foothills of the Andes - a town that has never had any rugby side tour there before. This gave an opportunity for Graham Tardif (President), Alan Skeats and Tim Griffin (Tour Manager and Assistant Tour Manager respectively) together with Rob Ryden (Captain) to air their views on local television.

The party of players consisted of Tim Benson, Matthew Brown, Ewan Clark, Jonathan Clark, Andy Cuthbert, Bill Davidson, Matt Dowse, Andy Evans, Ricky Forde, James Foster, Andrew Gardiner, Dougie Goodwin, Dougal Hawkes, Mick Hawkins, Kirk Heuser, Andrew Knox, Jon Lewis, Martin Livesey, Adrian McKay, Andy Maren, Keith Middleton, Simon Miller, Paul Southern and Jonathan Willis.

At San Juan we played Union San Juanina de Rugby and won handsomely before we took off on a marathon coach ride across the salt flats of northwest Argentina to a hotbed of tough rugby at Tucamen. It really was a hard match against Lince Rugby Club but a commendable 13-6 win was achieved.

Flying down to San Fernando on the River Plate, we were hosted at the Yacht Club in whose grounds was the pitch of Club San Fernando who we proceeded to beat. Finally back to Buenos Aires where our opponents were to be Club Athletico Lomas (affiliated to Richmond) and in wettish weather we struggled to a 16-14 victory.

Off again in 1993 for a second visit to South Africa to renew old friendships - some recorded in the 1976 report but now including Craig Jamieson, Harry Roberts, Fred Dieterle, Colin Formby, Elwyn Lloyd, Dennis Nick, Chris Ridl, Chris Saunders; all former Richmond players together with earlier Heavies namely Keith Oxlee, Mike van Zyl and Carel du Plessis not forgetting our former coach "Cocky" Crossley.

Tour Manager Alan Skeats had a splendid team including Director of Rugby Vinny Codrington, Dougie Goodwin (Club Captain), John Kingston (Coach) and Miriam Williams (Physiotherapist) while Andy Evans was on hand at every occasion to compile a video of the tour.

The players who touched down in Durban were Tim Benson, David Burns, Paul Carr, Jonathan Clark, David Clift, Andy Cuthbert, William Deeley, Phil Della-Savina, Matt Dowse, Martin Fairn, Steve Faktor, James Foster, Giles Goodburn, Paul Greenwood, Ian Grundy, Dougal Hawkes, Chris Hornung, Mike Hutton, Dean Jeffrey, Christopher Kays, Jonathan Lewis, Martin Livesey, Andy Maren, Damian Morris, Sean Phelan, Mark Roper, Eddie Saunders. Peter Smedley, Grant Taylor, Charles Wijeratna and Matt Yeldham.

The first match was floodlit against Durban Collegians and the result was a 16-16 draw, before the Hluhluwe Game Park beckoned again en route to a second floodlit game at Empangeni where Richmond won 41-13. Back up the road to Durban to catch a flight to Cape Town. There the first game ended in a win for us against Hamilton. The final game of the tour was in the pouring rain at another affiliated club, Villagers, and was another Richmond win.

So ended consistent touring, flying Richmond's flag in every continent and encouraging the playing of rugby union football in less developed rugby countries, until 2002 when the club reached out to new ground for us in Canada. With President Ian Botes captivating new friends, especially in high places - as the following message from Buckingham Palace will signify:

13th June 2002

"The Queen was pleased to receive your kind message of loyal greetings sent on behalf of Members of Richmond Football Club on the occasion of their Jubilee Tour to British Columbia, Canada which is being held from Friday until 24th June.
Her Majesty sends her best wishes for the enjoyment of your visit and the success of your matches."

With Andy Quigley (ex. Pink Floyd groupie) as Tour Manager, and poacher turned gamekeeper Andy Maren as Coach, success was bound to come. They were shored up by John Evans as Team Manager and Michelle Pearson as Physio.

A particularly hard fixture list had been assembled - and an itinerary which included four games in eight days meant that players had to exert every effort to overcome flight tiredness, rather lengthy evenings, high temperatures and opponents who included current Canadian internationals. All this was overcome when, at the Thunderbird Stadium, British Columbia R.U Under 21 XV were defeated 18-8, followed the next day by running out winners 30-20 over Meraloma Club at Bracton Oval, Stanley Park.

Two days of "rest" before Richmond took on Crimson Tide - Victoria Island representative XV at St Michael's University and won by 27-22 and then the final match back at Brocton Oval where our opponents were Capiland, and the tour ended with a convincing 34-19 win.

The players, under captain Andy Cuthbert, responsible for the splendid achievements were Rupert Alhusen, Alfie Ambrose, Ade Bamford, Oli Bishop, Martin Bolton, Matt Brown, Henry Buchanan, Chris Conway, Mark Draper, Ross Evans, Sean Flynn, Owen Gregory, Paul Harrison, Henry (Lord) Head, Zoran Higgins, Arthur Irving, Simon Lodder, Alex (Smiler) MacLennan, Mike (Pocket Rocket) McSweeney, Anthony Phillips, Tom Price, Ollie Quigley, James Samuel, Pieter Serfontein, Will (Chocolate) Taylor, Andy Warne, Chris (God) Whiteley, Paul Wilson and James (Tigger) Woods.

Chapter Nine

Women's Section

On Saturday 16 April 1986, The Athletic Ground staged the first women's rugby international match between Great Britain and France, the catalyst for the introduction of Richmond's own women's section.

Hearing of their dissatisfaction with the facilities at their Finchley base, a number of the English-based Great Britain players were invited to tea at The Savoy by the Richmond club. Suitably impressed by The Athletic Ground, Finchley's Jane Addey and Trisha (Moore) King called an Extraordinary General Meeting to propose a move to Richmond, which happened the following September.

Within a few months the squad had burgeoned and, when a second team was introduced, Richmond became first women's club in the world to run two teams. Richmond women had arrived - and with them came a pioneering spirit that was to carry them through the next two decades. In 2005/6, the club's 20th anniversary season, Richmond won the National Cup and the National Sevens Championship.

Ten Richmond players were in the original Great Britain team of 1986 and when, in 1987, Twickenham hosted its first ever women's game, Richmond competed on the hallowed turf in the Cup Final. Two years later, the West London women became the first to tour New Zealand. To this day, they remain the only side of any sex or age group in history to visit the islands and win every tour match (nine out of nine).

When the inaugural Women's World Cup (Cardiff, 1991) needed organising, four Richmond players formed the entire organising committee. When Scotland formed a team in 1993, Richmond team members were at the fore, and they helped to organise the World Cup of 1994 as well.

On the pitch, Richmond's women have achieved success unparalleled anywhere in the world. Twenty seasons have brought four European Sevens Championship titles, five National Premiership One crowns, Seven National Cup victories, five National Sevens titles and three Second Division successes.

Two of Richmond's Cup Final wins have been broadcast live on TV across the nation; the nail-biting victory over Clifton in 2001 at the Recreation Ground, Bath, and the thumping six try romp against Wasps at Twickenham in 2002.

For 17 seasons, the club has run three senior teams, all of which have had substantial winning records every season. In 2002/3 the club introduced a junior section. As a club, Richmond WRFC has played more matches (over 1,100), made more National Finals (14), scored more points (29,000 and rising), scored more tries (in excess of 5,000) and fielded more international players (74) than any other club in the world. At the last IRB Women's World Cup, there were 12 Richmond players competing for five countries.

Richmond's senior representative roll call makes impressive reading. Great Britain and England: Sue Dorrington, Pat Harris, Carol Isherwood, Alice Jenkinson, Jane Pauley, Janis Ross and Jayne Watts Great Britain and Wales: Janet Gedrych Great Britain, England and Scotland: Debbie Francis England: Teresa Andrews, Charlie Bronks, Jenny Chambers, Elizabeth Cribb, Nicola Coffin, Chris Diver, Emily Feltham, Karen Jones, Helen Flippance, Mary Forsyth, Kathy Jenn, Nicola Jupp, Nicola Meston, Deidre Mills, Jenny Phillips, Jo Poore, Julie Potter, Jackie Prout, Giselle Prangnell, Selena Rudge, Terri Siwek, Jenny Sutton, Rachel Vickers, Sarah Wenn and Sharon Whitehead. Ireland: Clare Hoppe, Diane Nixon, Raeltine Shrieves, Helen Siwek and Eryka Wessell Scotland: Alison Christie, Jen Dickson, Karen Findlay, Vicky Galbriath, Ali McGrandles, Erin Kerr, Lisa O'Keefe, Chris Ovenden, Claire Muir, Pogo Paterson, Jennifer Sheerin, Kath Vass and Victoria Wiseman. Wales: Sue Butler, Enid Davies, Heather Devine, Paula George, Dawn Mason, Wendy Shaw and Sue Thomas.

Countries further afield have also identified the prowess of Richmond women: for Australia, Alex Hargreaves; Canada, Kelly McCallum and Maureen MacMahon; Holland, Anna Van Wareren; Italy, Maria Tondinelli; Japan, Runa Hattori; Kazahkstan, Ellfita Tamayera; New Zealand, Rochelle Martin and Anna Richards; Spain, Rosa Calafat, Montse Martin and Rocio Ramirez; Sweden, Maria Nordstrom and Louise Vaerlien; and the U.S.A, Lisa Weix.

Like the men in the club, the women enjoy their touring. The distinctive black, red and gold hoops have travelled the globe, playing in Italy, France, New Zealand, Spain, Holland, the USA and Scotland. In 2005, they became the first international women's club to visit South Africa. The team was welcomed with a drinks reception at the British Consulate in Pretoria and went on to win all four tour games, including the key test against South Africa's national club champions, the Goodwood Gazelles.

There have been many special seasons, but two stand out. In 1990 (when the Richmond WRFC third XV started out), the first and second team won all 26 of their respective league games. The club played 62 games in all and won a remarkable and unprecedented 58 times, scoring 1841 points and conceding a mere 183. This represents a match average of 30 points to three. The only defeat suffered by the second team all season was at the hands of their first team rivals, in the semi final of the National Cup.

In 1995, Richmond fielded sides boasting players who have captained Wales, Scotland, England, Great Britain, Ireland, New Zealand, Spain, Holland, the Nomads and The Classic Lionesses. That year, the first team played 22 matches, winning them all (as well as the league and cup double). They scored a record breaking 802 points, conceding just 48. In the six months between October and March the side did not concede a single point.

The first twenty years have been packed with pioneering people and performances. The aspiration is always to maintain the club's prized reputation at the forefront of women's rugby across the globe.

Club Landmarks

- In 1986/7 the first women's captain, Mary Forsyth, and her team gained their first honours, winning the National Sevens. Under Dee Mills, they won the National League title a season later.

- In 1998/9, Carol Isherwood and Pat Harris led Richmond to victory in the National Cup and the National Sevens

- Debbie Francis's side took the championship of the National League in 1990/1 before winning the National Cup the following year.

- In 1993/4 Mary Harrington's side added to the silverware by taking the National Cup once more.

- In 1994/5 the team, led by Sue Butler, put two more 'pots' on display, winning the National League and the National Cup.

- At the end of the 1995/96 season, prop Karen Findlay led a team to National Sevens victory. Karen's team carried on to take the National League trophy the following year.

- In 1999/2000 Nicky Coffin's team won the National Sevens and the National Cup, which they went on to regain in 2002.

- In 1999 Richmond's second team achieved glory in the Amsterdam International Sevens Tournament, an honour that they went on to retain for a further three years.

- In 2002/3, a Junior Academy was set up and the 1st XV finished second in National Premiership One and, a year later, the 3rd XV was named the Impalas.

- 2004/5 saw distinction in the short game when two Richmond 7s teams reached the final of the Stoneygate Sevens.

- In 2005/6 under the leadership of Nicki Drinkwater (Jupp) and Dawn Mason, Richmond became National Cup winners for a record seventh time, adding the National Sevens title by defeating Saracens and avenging their loss of the Premiership One crown.

Chapter Ten

Youth Development

Richmond has always been at the forefront of youth rugby - many years ahead of other clubs - and took the lead with London Scottish in 1923/4 when the inaugural match between schoolboys representing both clubs was played at the New Year. These games involved players from most of the leading public schools, eventually producing "gates" in their thousands each year and attended by leading national press rugby reporters. These gentlemen attempted to spot boys who would later make their mark at senior clubs and international level. Of these there were many - not only for the two Athletic Ground clubs but for other major clubs in the United Kingdom. These high profile games continued into the nineteen eighties but then ceased, regrettably, largely due to the prohibitive cost of bringing schoolboys from Scotland to field the London Scottish XV.

There was a revival on 1st January 2003 when a Richmond Student Under 21 XV beat a similar London Scottish side 22-0 and this has now become a regular seasonal feature.

In addition to these fixtures, Richmond had, in the 1950s, encouraged an annual Spring match between Schoolmasters and Schoolboys and commenced Colts fixtures with other London clubs. These games also provided stars of the future, not only on the rugby field but also in other spheres. Two names spring to mind - Lord Archer, a fast winger from Wellington School, Somerset, and another whose acting abilities will be known to all - David Suchet.

The Colts XV continued each season until 1981/2 with the addition, in 1972/3, of an under 23 side.

It was at this time that Graham Tardif used to coach Richmond youngsters joining in with those from London Scottish on Sunday mornings and, at the end of the 80/1 season, Graham told Simon Codrington that he would split from the co-tenants the following year and go it alone. Simon, armed with the records of Graham who had relocated to Bermuda, took over the reins and attended a meeting of Middlesex mini-rugby organisers in Ruislip where he found that our efforts were "amateurish" when compared with London Irish who, even then, had managers, coaches and bag handlers for every age group. So that blueprint was installed in our club and in 1982/3 the club first officially recognised mini-rugby and also fielded an Under 19 team. That the system was good was proved when Richmond won the Middlesex Under 11s competition.

Help for Simon Codrington was given by his brother Vinny, Wyn Ellis, Pat

Lavery, Peter Quinnen, Brian Taylor, Nigel Wilson and Peter Bray whose particular remit was to identify fathers who could be recruited to the organisation. However, there were difficulties, not least the non-availability of the Golf Driving Range area on Sunday mornings and the reluctance of the Ground Manager to open the clubhouse at those times, which led to the squeezing of ever-growing numbers of boys into a restricted area.

The father recruitment went well, even enlisting old stagers like Ian Botes, David Buchanan and Chris Ralston, and new teams emerged with an Under 13 in 1983/4 and, a year later, an Under 14 XV. Meanwhile, after the Colts season in 1981/2, that side was re-designated Under 21 and ran for four years with a re-emergence for two years in 1988/9 and 89/90. Earlier, 1985/6 had seen the birth of the Under 15 team and a year later the Under 16s.

In 1989 the Colts took the field again, alongside all the other age groups, for two years before they split into Colts and Colts Under 17. At the beginning of the nineties, the current pattern of Under 19, 17, 16, 15, 14, 13 and Mini-Rugby was established and, although small changes have seen in 1998/9 with an Academy/Under 21 XV, and the re-introduction of the Colts, this pattern still continues. In 1999/2000 the Colts were the leading junior side, followed by U17s down to U13s and, of course, the essential mini-rugby. The last two years have seen the older sides designated Academy and U19 and, after the early days of building up such an important youth base, mention must be made of the following members who contributed largely to the success story and these are: Mike Andersen, Charlie Armour, Ted Aves, "Dinger" Bell, Simon Everton, Colin Holman, Chris Holt, John Houlton, Roger Lewis, Polys Pateras, Robert Rakison and Rocky Skinner, although without doubt the largest single contributor in various capacities has been Andy Quigley.

It might be thought that enlarging the club's scope and spreading the youth policy was a largely Sunday morning effort but this section, like the others in the club, has embraced competitions over the British Isles and Eire and undertaken tours as far afield as the Antipodes.

The main tournaments from age six years old have been Middlesex County, London Irish, Staines and the world's largest at Worthing. At all of these Richmond has won individual age groups and gained the accolade of "Most Successful Club" which, at some venues, means not only gaining the most wins but also being the best behaved. Particular achievements have been three youth sides winning the Middlesex County Cup in 1993 and collecting that County's Under 19 Cup in 1995 with a victory over Harlequins, with leading sides London Irish, Saracens and Wasps being also-rans. This last title was achieved again in 1998 with London Irish being the losers.

The following year, in spite of the trauma in the club's senior side,

Richmond's Under 21 team landed the first ever National Championship at that age group, defeating Harlequins in the final. Many of these junior sides form the bedrock of today's successful 1st XV. In 2000/1 the Under 14s triumphed in their age group National Championship at Twickenham.

By the early nineteen nineties, youth was spreading its wings in Devon, Cornwall and South Wales where the opposition included Dunvant and Llanelli. In 1996, Richmond took in its largest tour in terms of numbers with two hundred boys in four buses to Paris and Caen where historic World War II sites were visited.

Even in the days of administration, the spirit was not quelled and one hundred and forty boys from the Under 19s, 17s, 16s and 15s made a successful foray to Cape Town and Durban. Following that period of uncertainty, to quote Andy Quigley, "the Mini and Youth sections, along with their parents, carried on stoically as if nothing had changed. The club owes a great deal of gratitude for the support at that time."

To bring events up-to-date, it must be recorded that in the last season the Under 17s came back from the rugby strongholds of Australia, Fiji and New Zealand with a hundred per cent record and, in 2004, the Under 16s performed strongly in South Africa.

In 2004/5 all age groups continued to flourish with the highlights being the Under 13's tour to the Lot Valley in France and the Under 17's success in claiming the Surrey Championship for the third time in five years.

As well as aping their seniors on the field and abroad, the Minis have staged the extremely successful Richmond Mini Rugby Tournament embracing teams from all over the country and the annual Minis Dinner has become a permanent and joyful fixture on the club's social calendar.

Chapter Eleven

Run-Up to Professionalism

Although rugby union embraced professionalism in 1995, reportedly at the insistence of the Antipodean members of the International Board, the game in England, perhaps not consciously, had been moving towards that sort of structure since 1969.

This was when the Bristol Club convened a meeting which was to lead to Merit Tables, Leagues (a dirty word at RFU Twickenham!) and Cups - therefore providing a platform, together with the sponsorship that had emerged, for the game to be placed on a total financial footing.

The meeting referred to was called to discuss points on which leading clubs were at issue with the R.F.U and the first one of these instanced (can you believe it now?) too much live television coverage thus depleting gates and bar revenue and the need for (in some shape) a club competition.

Secondly, it was felt that, because of the role of the Constitutional Bodies (ie. The Counties), the senior clubs had inadequate representation on the Rugby Football Union and there existed a need for a Major Clubs' Sub-committee to meet regularly with officials at Twickenham.

The third contention was that falling standards in the game required a call for the reduction of excessive calls upon players and the elimination of the County Championship in its then current form.

These proposals were accepted by Richmond together with thirty-nine other clubs and led to the establishment of the Gate Taking Clubs Association, as the only invitees to the meeting were those clubs which charged for admission to their ground.

Regular meetings (much to the chagrin of the R.F.U at that time) took place and the club was represented by Mike Humphreys, Tony Vyvyan and Alan Skeats.

This meeting spawned the setting up of regional committees in the Midlands, North and South-West to run alongside that of London which had been allowed since the early nineteen sixties to have its own group on which sat Frank Bisgood and, later, Alan Skeats until 1993 for Richmond.

Opposition to the fact that the leading clubs now had a national mouthpiece continued to come from the Constituent Bodies but pressure was building and, in 1974, the R.F.U. initiated the Mallaby Committee, chaired by Sir George Mallaby, to consider the future of the game in England. Richmond were honoured by the selection of Tony Vyvyan as a committee member. An old friend of Richmond, Budge Rogers also served.

Time moved on with the leading clubs having re-titled themselves the Senior Clubs Association with an Executive comprising two members from each region and Alan Skeats was one of the London Delegates. In 1976, it was agreed by all parties to form a Major Clubs Sub-Committee of the R.F.U. and, for the first two years, Tony Vyvyan was again fighting the senior clubs corner in those meetings.

Things continued to evolve and gradual expansion under the R.F.U. meant that two sub-committees had delegates from the major clubs' regional committees. These were the Competition Sub-Committee and the Senior Clubs' Sub-Committee on the latter of which London was represented by Alan Skeats until 1993.

Alongside all these happenings, the clubs had a National Cup, then local, and later, national Merit Tables before the hitherto obscene word "leagues" passed the lips of the R.F.U.

So, from the inception in 1969 of a think-tank for the leading clubs until the onset of salaries for players when the Union Sub-Committees ceased to exist and so to the Senior Club's Committees, it will be seen that Richmond was always involved.

Chapter Twelve

Professional Era and Aftermath - Administration

As recorded in Chapter Four, professional rugby was ordained by the International Board on 27th August 1995 and, in September 1995, Richmond began to come to terms with the funding required to finance such an enterprise, even though the club was then in Division Three.

A discussion had been heard by the brother of former Richmond players in which two solicitors were discussing which rugby club their client should invest in after having become interested in rugby through junior club Winchester. Their discussion was interrupted by the listener who suggested Richmond might answer their problem.

The upshot was that the then Director of Rugby, Vinny Codrington, was contacted and met these legal men in London where he outlined the history of the club, its background and the position of The Athletic Ground.

Next day, Vinny was asked if he would travel at short notice to meet the intended investor and, after having agreed, he was contacted again the following day and asked to be at Battersea Heliport at 9.30am on the following Sunday morning.

David Buchanan, as President, agreed with the arrangement with the proviso that Michael Hess as Chairman for the Executive should be kept in the picture and it was agreed that Tony Dorman should also travel on this trip. At the same time, Vinny advised John Kingston of the impending developments immediately prior to our match at Rotherham.

The route of the journey was by helicopter to Blackbushe Airport to board a six-seater Lear jet (the solicitors were also on board) bound for Nice from where another helicopter flew them to Monaco heliport - thence on to a Monte Carlo apartment. This turned out to be the home of Ashley Levett who had acquired wealth by copper trading in the City of London.

Further discussions took place which also encompassed the club's association with London Scottish. A lunch at a restaurant opposite the Casino followed before the return journey. During the following week Ashley Levett expressed his interest and Vinny informed Mike Hess and Martin Slagter of the situation. With David Buchanan, it was agreed that the matter should be on the agenda at the next Executive meeting, when it was agreed that the dialogue should continue.

Ashley Levett appointed Symon Elliott to attend the bi-weekly meetings and Robert Rakison was brought in to provide legal protection for Richmond. It was emphasised that Richmond's heritage was of
paramount importance and agreed that club members would be able to appoint two directors to the board with veto rights over defined heritage

matters. Messrs Hess and Buchanan were nominated for this role.

Discussions continued and it emerged that Ben Clarke was willing to join. This gave enormous impetus to the possibility of 'high level' professionalism at Richmond.

All the ongoing discussions came to a head at an Extraordinary General Meeting of the club in May 1996 when Ashley Levett took the chair and expounded his plans to make Richmond the best side in Europe within five years. His parting words to a well-attended assembly of a club with £30,000 in the bank were that "you have my word that, whatever happens, I will leave Richmond in no worse state than I found it." The upshot was that, after intense questioning, the members overwhelmingly committed themselves to the project. Ashley Levett then agreed to inject £2.5 million equity capital in the first 8 months, giving him 81% control after a rights issue in early 1997.

With the deal done, player recruitment proceeded apace. Virtually all the successful 3rd division-winning team members were offered contracts to continue - either as a part-time professional or an amateur. Big names began to appear - Adrian Davies and Andy Moore, Welsh caps from Cardiff, Scott Quinnell from Wigan for a record-breaking transfer fee of £250,000 - soon to be followed by his younger brother, Craig. Signings included Richard West, Jim Fallon, Brian Moore (from Harlequins and England), Darren Crompton, Simon Mason (Irish international). Later, Alan Bateman, the former Welsh centre, joined from rugby league in Australia and was to revive his international rugby union career.

During the summer of 1996, Vinny Codrington secured a substantial 3-year sponsorship with Oracle but, in late 1996, he sensed a serious decline in his relationship with Symon Elliott and decided to leave at the end of the season. A number of members too, were starting to become disillusioned because, in spite of heritage promises, things were changing. There was the dropping Richmond's famous old gold, red and black in favour of a 'modern' red and black strip. The club's traditional badge had gone and a garish logo introduced on all the stationery. Home matches were accompanied by a high decibel cacophony of sound on the loudspeaker which, with a pop song, lauded our scores but was uncivilly quiet when the opposition registered points.

The first season saw Richmond battling it out with Newcastle for the key promotion spot in Division 2. Richmond had built up a squad of 32 players including many internationals. One of the first professional games at The Athletic Ground featured Sir John Hall's Newcastle, led by Rob Andrew. Over 6000 spectators wanted to see the match, as over 20 internationals were included in the teams. The gates had to be shut and there were ticket touts operating up and down the A316.

The season went well, Richmond achieved promotion to the First Division and, despite the already apparent financial pressures, Richmond and London Scottish, via the RAA, managed to spend £260,000 on turning the famous Long Bar into a themed all-sports bar - which meant that another piece of our heritage had gone. At the end of that season, when Richmond had finished 5th, there was another hint that events were not going to schedule off the field. Symon Elliott, Ashley Levett's nominee, suddenly departed in March 1998. The budget was out of control and there were other setbacks as Richmond Borough Council had objected to the permanent erection of, in their view, the unsightly temporary stand and corporate hospitality suites at the west end of the ground.

Tony Hallett became Chief Executive having, with David Buchanan, now become one the club's two nominee directors. Peter Moore, who had been a Richmond member since 1970 and who had been part of the new team since October 1996 as General Manager, became Company Secretary.

In the first two seasons the club lost over £5 million, all of which had been provided by Ashley Levett. It was clear that one of the only ways to increase revenue was to increase ground capacity. Richmond Borough Council had restricted The Athletic Ground to 5,900 spectators and, in order to break even, Richmond needed 8,000 for home matches.

Heritage then lost out again as, after presentations to 'key club members', the club moved to play 1998-9 home matches at the newly-built 25,000 seater Madjedski Stadium in Reading. Here, Ashley Levett (in spite of advice from people with a rugby background) averred, we would attract gates of 15,000 (from 'the rugby hungry Thames Valley') - but only Leicester had ever approached this figure. In fact the club did remarkably well and opened the season at Madjedski with a 10,000 crowd and a win over Newcastle.

By this time, the Board was already beginning to cut costs and would have sold Agustin Pichot to Leicester for a six figure sum, but they had not told the player who, when he heard, responded that he was not a "piece of meat to be bought and sold." He came to England to play for Richmond.

John Kingston also had his budget cut - the players could no longer claim win bonuses and were asked to take a 10% pay reduction. After a defeat by Gloucester during which Craig Quinnell and Barry Williams were sin-binned, Ashley informed the players that there would be a two week pay fine for every sinbin, a four week pay fine for a second offence and a six week pay fine for a sending-off.

On 27 February 1999 we played Leicester in the quarter-final of the Tetley Bitter Cup and, due to John Kingston's strategy of playing the Tigers at their own game - up front, we achieved a tremendous upset with a 15-13 win - but Ashley Levett was not there to see it. Twenty four hours earlier, at a Board Meeting, he had declined to continue his financial support. John Kingston knew this before the cup game but had not told the players.

The Board Meeting had been called in order to sign off the 1997-8 financial accounts for Richmond FC Ltd as these needed to be filed at Companies House by March 31st. The audit partner was also present. As the company was losing money, the major issue to be considered was whether the company was a 'going concern' i.e. could the company meet obligations as they fell due. The budget for 1998-9 showed another loss - now down to approximately £1 million. The only way of covering this was for Ashley Levett to agree to underwrite this amount. Ashley declined to do so, at which point his nominee directors, Robin Hutson and Walton Eddleston, resigned. The remaining Board Members - Tony Hallett, Tony Dorman and John Fenton, followed their legal duty to take proper legal advice and took the only correct option a vailable which was to seek the protection of the court, placing the company into Administration on March 8th 1999, so that: -

a) RFC could fulfil its remaining premiership fixtures
b) RFC had time to refinance and restructure
c) RFC would not be at risk of individual creditors serving a winding-up petition.

- also, there would be more time to find potential new investors.

Even in this dire hour, hope was eternal on the hearts of some and both Tony Dorman and Tony Hallett pledged £20,000 each plus additional funds from other closely-involved members to start a fighting fund. Peter Moore waived his salary but, meanwhile, the Administrators, who now had total control, asked for a list of players to be sacked. Further wage reductions were made, also ruthless cuts throughout the club and the offices in Parkshot that Richmond had rented were closed.

Things were no better at co-tenants, London Scottish. In early 1999, London Scottish's principal investor had sold a 24% stake to Bristol with an option to buy the rest of the equity. Bristol needed a First Division club to take over as insurance against failing to win promotion and a place in the Premiership in 1999/2000 and had agreed to fund London Scottish for the remainder of the season - Tony Tiarks was running out of money too...

Ashley Levett attended the home match in March v Bath but was shunned by the players. Other clubs starting approaching our players but all remained loyal. Our remaining fixtures were fulfilled, helped out by the fighting fund and Agustin Pichot, who stumped up £350 for a team bus on one occasion - Ben Clarke's parents also helped out and we completed the season, finishing 9th in the premiership.

Meanwhile, new investors had made pledges of support but the bubble burst some weeks later when they learnt that English First Division Rugby (EFDR) had offered £500,000 to the Administrators for Richmond's share in EFDR Ltd in order to exclude the club from the Premiership. The retraction was due also to a statement by the owner of Gloucester, Tom Walkinshaw and Chairman of EFDR that, unless the offer was accepted, a clause in the EFDR Ltd articles would be invoked to allow the Premiership clubs to buy Richmond's share for one pound -

an interpretation which, at best, was doubtful.

Our "friends" in the Premiership clubs, most of which we had played against for many years, raised no voice in support of Richmond and, because of the determination to reduce the league from fourteen to twelve clubs, a deal was concocted to merge Richmond and London Scottish with London Irish. Indeed, at a meeting leading up to our isolation, Tony Dorman had been told by the EFDR Chairman , "I have a mandate from the clubs to throw you out". This was in spite of the fact that the earlier "Mayfair Agreement" stipulated that twelve months notice should be given before any move to reduce the number of clubs in the premiership. As the owner of Northampton, Keith Barwell, said "there is only so much room in the lifeboat and the weak must be thrown overboard."

Readers today should understand that the First Division (now becoming the 'Premier League') had been increased from twelve to fourteen clubs for the 1998-9 season as a short-term reaction to problems with what is now known as the Heineken Cup. The English clubs had pulled out, increasing the size of the First Division to fourteen to overcome the fixture shortfall, but then rejoined Europe, needing to reduce the league to twelve clubs again.

In the months that followed, all kinds of propositions hit the headlines and rumours abound - but the simple truth was that the determination to reduce the size of the division was absolute and Richmond's weakness made it an ideal target. Buchler Phillips pointed out that EFDR ignored a relevant wording in its clauses which states that a club can enter into Administration "for the purposes of a reconstruction" which was the aim when Richmond entered this process.

The cruel fact remained that, by ignoring the law and its own wordings, EFDR opportunistically achieved its objectives of reducing the number of clubs for the 1999/2000 season from fourteen to twelve.

So the die was cast; Premiership Rugby had abandoned us and we were later to find that the Rugby Football Union and our Constituent Body, Middlesex were not interested in our wellbeing. We were to be swept under the carpet, if possible. The suspicion was that some diehards in the RFU and Middlesex were secretly pleased to see Richmond's problems and to use them as a lesson for those choosing the professional route.

Goodbye to Madjedski Stadium, the Premiership and Ashley Levett's seven million and hello to the Administrators and no future as a single club, for it had been 'agreed' somewhere in the corridors of power that, along with London Scottish, we should be merged with London Irish. A new company set up by London Irish received £1,500,000 from EFDR/RFU to expedite this - funding which had been offered by EFDR to any clubs willing to merge or accept relegation before Richmond's 'broken wing' became apparent. London Irish incorporated some of the colours of Richmond and our co-tenants, as a consequence of a sale agreement whereby the Administrator sold our share in EFDR for £149,000 plus £1,000 for 'intellectual property rights' and the upshot was London Irish were £1.5m better off, even though Richmond never agreed to this deal.

Meanwhile, back at the club, members Tony Dorman, Tony Hallett, Richard Humphrey and Peter Moore set to work, building a team to ensure that Richmond could continue as an independent club. Richmond Vikings Limited (RVL) was formed to act as the rescue vehicle.

Then a new threat arrived in the shape of a bid from Ken Bates of Chelsea Football Club who started discussions with the RFC Administrator and London Scottish RAA directors seeking to purchase, by way of assignment, the lease of The Athletic Ground. Chelsea needed a new training ground but did not require the full area and would not agree to a continuation of amateur rugby on those parts of the ground not required for soccer training. The Chelsea offer was over two million pounds so this was a massive challenge and major threat. A further members' meeting agreed to raise funds to safeguard Richmond's interest in the RAA and to enable us to continue as an amateur club. Hallett, as a director of the RAA, ably assisted by Richard Humphrey and with the support of the RFC Administrator, thwarted Chelsea and Tiarks, the major London Scottish shareholder, to retain the lease within RAA.

Time moved on to July 1999 and the Administrators agreed that Richmond Football Club Ltd (in Administration) would accept a bid from Richmond Vikings Ltd (RVL) in the sum of £250,000 for the club's debenture ticket rights. The funds raised from these tickets were a significant help in our recovery. The fundraising continued in earnest with our Head of Sponsorship, Richard Humphrey, co-ordinating the effort. Committee structures were reformed and, under Vic Balchin, fixtures (outside the leagues as we had none to play in) were negotiated - although discussions with the RFU on our future role in the leagues continued via Richard Humphrey and Peter Moore. Other involved members at the time included Andy Quigley, Harry Hooper, Neil Aitken, Jen Gadsby Peet, Simon Everton, Charlie Armour, Andy Cuthbert and 'Dinger' Bell.

Donations, even at that early stage, had reached not far short of £200,000 and Richard Humphreys' Herculean efforts not only had a response from members but from very many well-wishers outside the club - including a generous donation from Tony O' Reilly - at that time characteristically anonymous but something the club would like, now, to acknowledge.

In September, Dorman, Hallett and Moore agreed with Buchler Phillips that RVL would purchase Richmond's 49% interest in the RAA, RFCL goodwill and inter-company debt for £725,000 with a non-refundable deposit of a third of the sum payable immediately and the balance due in March 2000. Six months only to find another £475,000 to ensure we survived!

The efforts of all those named earlier continued and, in late 1999, a new hero joined them. David Corben, who had played for Old Paulines, was also a

Richmond member and had heard of our plight from Andy Quigley and Tony Hallett, came aboard to help with the rescue. He also became Chairman of RVL with Peter Moore as Financial Director. RVL was now properly capitalised and the four major shareholders injected over £600,000 by way of equity and interest-free loans.

In March 2000, Tony Tiarks, the backer of London Scottish, tried yet again - demanding an Extraordinary General Meeting of the RAA with the intention of casting 49% of the votes held by London Scottish together with Richmond's 49% (held, he thought, by the Administrator) to allow Chelsea Football Club to take over The Athletic Ground lease. The meeting was called at the ungodly hour of 09:00, presumably to obviate any chance of the minority two percent of the RAA shareholders being present. In the event, Richmond (RVL) was in control of its 49% and, in any case, a 75% majority was required - the would-be sellers had not read the articles.

Soon after this, the difficult position between Ashley Levett and Richmond FC was resolved when he agreed to sell his Richmond Football Club Ltd shares to RVL for £1. He also assigned the return due on the the club's debt to him personally from the Administrator to Richmond Vikings Ltd for £120,000, plus 50% of any amount in excess of that which he subsequently waived. This could be seen as generous under the circumstances - but did it fulfil his promise to that first EGM 'not to leave the club in a worse state than when he found it'?

Readers and observers of Richmond FC history must judge.

Fundraising was not over because London Scottish's 49% ownership of the RAA was in doubt as Bristol had put London Scottish Ventures into receivership. In July 2000, Richmond Vikings decided to buy the share - with our co-tenants or alone. Two months later, it became obvious that London Scottish could not raise the necessary cash whilst we were becoming financially stronger day-by-day.

In October 2000, the bid process for the purchase of the L.S 49% share of the RAA was contractually agreed. A month later the deal was completed with Richmond Football Club Ltd (RFC) owing 98% (effectively all) of Richmond Athletic Association Ltd shares - the principal asset being the lease of the ground. This required further loan funding by the major shareholders.

Subsequently, London Scottish agreed a sub-lease to continue to play at The Athletic Ground ranking equally with Richmond until the existing lease runs out in 2016. This was announced when we played them in March 2001, a match attended by over two thousand spectators - a gate exceeding those at many national league grounds.

It was resolved in September 2001 that Richmond's rugby objective is the National Leagues and an evolving infrastructure has been put in place to achieve that goal. It was also recorded that, in December of the same year, membership numbers exceeded 2,000. In March 2002, the High Court approved the formal exit of Richmond Football Club Ltd from Administration.

So, in the space of just seven years, the club had employed some of the finest players, been funded by millions of pounds, crashed to near oblivion and been rescued by the sterling efforts by club members who raised over £1.4 million for the rescue. Richmond FC stands ready now, in good financial heart, to climb the rungs, making friends in every league it passes through, playing again proudly in its Old Gold, Red and Black colours.

Chapter Thirteen

The Future Outlook

With the club in a stable financial position and maintaining a very strong squad base on the playing side, bolstered by recruitment and the development of our youth XVs, the future looks good for promotion over the next few seasons.

However, although not quite the "Sword of Damocles", there is a looming problem with The Athletic Ground itself. This was instanced first in a report compiled by the London Borough of Richmond-upon-Thames back in April 1998.

The gist of this report, part of an overall look at the whole Crown-owned land area adjacent to Old Deer Park, is that our playing area should incorporate uninterrupted views to the west and north, reflecting the historical nature of the area.

This would place restrictions on the amount of car parking to 347 places in areas properly accessed and landscaped. Additionally, the amount of floodlighting and the volume of loudspeakers should be limited.

Although as a listed building, the old pavilion will remain, the 1958 grandstand is regarded as unsightly and interrupts views across the park and the proposal is that a new structure should be constructed on the site of the existing golf-driving range and its design should include the functions of many smaller buildings which would disappear.

This would mean re-siting of the main pitch and it is understood that these suggestions are approved by the land owners, the Crown Commissioners, and will be subject to their granting of a renewal lease to the R.A.A beyond 2016.

Plans and negotiations have been drawn up but the tempo is at last quickening (2006) and it is envisaged that the time period on this project is now relatively short term.

Perhaps the next history will be written in a special archives room in the new grandstand complex.

Chapter Fourteen

R.A.A Directors 1961 - 2002

The Richmond Athletic Association was set up in 1885 to operate the Crown Lease on The Athletic Ground and the founder members were Richmond F.C, London Scottish F.C, Richmond Cricket Club and the Richmond Horse Show. The last two founders ceased to function at the ground many years ago and the two rugby clubs had 49% shares each with the remaining two per cent being held by individuals. Following the administration of Richmond and the liquidation of London Scottish, all but the individual 2% of shares have been held by our club i.e 98%.

Richmond's directors on the board since 1961 have been:

ALLAN, Colin	1968 - 70
BISGOOD, Frank	1961 - 80
BLACK, John	1961 - 72
BOTES, Ian	1991 - 93
CARNABY, Bill	1981 - 86
CASTLE, John	1980
CLARKE, Geoff	1983 - 89
CODRINGTON, Vinny	1993 - 97
CORBEN, David	2000 - continuing
CORMACK, Arthur	1961 - *
CORMACK, George	1970 - 74
CRESSWELL, Keith	1989 - 91
ELLIOTT, Symon	1996 - 98
HALLETT, Tony	1998 - continuing
HESS, Michael	1991 - 93
HOLT, Chris	1994 - 97
HUMPHREYS, Michael	1986 - 96
JUDD, Murray	1979 - 83
LOVELL, Fred	1961 - 64
MOORE, Peter	1997 - 98
	2000-continuing
O'BRIEN, R.H "Horse"	1961 - 70
PAGE, Andrew	1966 - 69
PATERAS, "Polys"	1993 - 95

PEARCE, Bernard	1986 - 88
PINNINGTON, Neville	1963
POWELL-REES, John	1963 - 65
QUINNEN, Nigel	1981 - 87
QUINNEN, Peter	1992 - 93
RAKISON, Robert	1989 - 91
RIDER, Tom	1970 - *
RILEY, John	1964 - 87
SHARP, Antony	1982 - 86
SKEATS, Alan	1969 - 91
SLAGTER, Martin	1995 - 97
STANSFIELD, Tony	1981 - 92
STOY, Fred	1980 - 92
TARDIF, Graham	- 81 *
VALLINGS, Robert	1991 - 97
VYVYAN, Tony	1968 - 82
WATES, Ted	1967

* Records incomplete due to missing documents.

1st XV MATCH STATISTICS
(except Major Tours fixtures)

Year	Played	Won	Lost	Drawn	For	Against
1961/2	34	22	11	1	528	267
1962/3	22	12	10	0	247	206
1963/4	29	20	9	0	513	230
1964/5	33	23	10	0	502	293
1965/6	31	21	8	2	427	273
1966/7	36	22	11	3	521	282
1967/8	29	17	11	1	402	278
1968/9	27	11	15	1	313	307
1969/70	34	15	19	0	388	448
1970/1	29	7	20	2	292	415
1971/2	34	17	16	1	539	541
1972/3	35	18	16	1	601	580
1973/4	33	18	13	2	533	445
1974/5	32	22	9	1	467	323
1975/6	34	20	13	1	502	490
1976/7	32	14	17	1	442	418
1977/8	32	18	12	1	401	367
1978/9	28	12	13	3	376	381
1979/80	32	12	18	2	453	524
1980/1	32	8	23	1	320	468
1981/2	33	16	16	1	459	383
1982/3	32	10	21	1	393	516
1983/4	33	15	17	1	519	591
1984/5	29	12	17	0	493	602
1985/6	30	11	18	1	486	540
1986/7	34	16	18	0	537	720
1987/8	33	12	19	2	411	602
1988/9	31	12	17	2	413	555
1989/90	35	22	10	3	717	509
1990/1	32	10	20	2	447	616
1991/2	30	19	10	1	601	475
1992/3	34	19	14	1	806	628
1993/4	31	14	17	0	667	560
1994/5	34	17	16	1	695	581

1995/6	34	26	7	1	1,096	604
1996/7	32	27	4	1	1,461	619
1997/8*	38	23	15	0	1,039	794
1998/9	33	17	14	2	840	793
1999/2000	21	14	7	0	635	388
2000/1	30	28	2	0	1,262	168
2001/2	31	30	1	0	1,611	228
2002/3	27	26	1	0	1,249	186
2003/4	28	26	2	0	1,225	269
2004/5	28	20	8	0	823	360
2005/6	28	22	6	0	1,003	438

* 1997/8 No record of points in first four matches.

Decade-by-decade Summary

1961/70	275	163	104	8	3,841	2,584
1970/80	321	158	147	15	4,606	4,484
1980/90	322	134	176	12	4,748	5,486
1992/00	319	186	124	9	8,287	6,058
2000/06	172	152	20	0	7,173	1,649
	1,409	793	571	44	28,655	20,261

League Positions

Season	League	Position
1980/1	London Merit Table	5
1981/2	London Merit Table	8
1982/3	London Merit Table	9
1983/4	London Merit Table	6
1984/5	London Merit Table	9
1985/6	John Smith Table B	10
1986/7	John Smith Table B	2
1987/8	National 2	6
1988/9	National 2	9
1989/90	National 2	3
1990/1	National 2	12 R
1991/2	National 3	1 P
1992/3	National 2	9 R
1993/4	National 3	7
1994/5	National 3	8
1995/6	National 3	2 P
1996/7	National 2	1 P
1997/8	National 1/Premiership	5
1998/9	Premiership	9
1999/2000	Did not compete	
2000/1	Herts/Middlesex 1	1 P
2001/2	London 4 South West	1 P
2002/3	London 3 South West	1 P
2003/4	London 2 South	1 P
2004/5	London 1	3
2005/6	London 1	2

P = Promotion
R = Relegation

1st XV Opponents (excluding major tours)

Abbey
Aberavon
Alton
Andover
Army
Askeans
Bagneres
Ballymena
Banca Nationale (Argentina)
Barnstaple
Barnes
Basingstoke
Bath
Beckingham
Bedford
Birmingham
Bishop's Stortford
Blackheath
Blaydon
Bracknell
Bridgend
Bridgewater & Albion
Bristol
Brixham
Broughton Park
Bulldogs (South Africa)
Camberley
Camborne
Cambridge
Cambridge University
Canterbury
Cardiff
Cheshunt
Chicago (USA)
Chobham
Civil Service
Clifton
Clontarf

Club Athletic Lomas (Argentina)
Club Universitaire de Rugby
(Paraguay)
Cobham
Colomiers
Combined Services
Cork Constitution
Coventry
Cranleigh
Cross Keys
Croydon & District
Davenport
Diss
Doncaster
Dorking
Ealing
East Africa
Eastern Suburbs (Australia)
Ebbw Vale
Effingham & Leatherhead
Enfield Ignations
Esher
Exeter
Exeter University
Falmouth
Farnborough
Farnham
Feltham
Finchley
Flyde
Gakushi (Japan)
Guernsey
Glamorgan Wanderers
Gloucester
Gosforth (Newcastle Gosforth)
Gosport & Fareham
Grasshoppers
Grenoble

Guildford & Godalming
Guildfordians
Guys Hospital
Halifax
Harlequins
Harlow
Harrogate
Harrow
Havant
Hawick
Haywards Heath
Headingley
Henley
Heriots FP
Hertford
High Wycombe
International XX
Jersey
Kendal
Law Society
Lensbury
Leicester
Lewes
Le Zebre (South Africa)
Lince (Argentina)
Liverpool St Helens
Llanelly (Llanelli)
London Irish
London Kiwis
London New Zealand
London Nigerians
London Scottish
London University
London Welsh
Lydney
Maesteg
Matson
Metropolitan Police
Middlesborough
Mill Hill
Morley

Moseley
Neath
Newbridge
New Brighton
Newbury
New Milton
Newport
New South Wales (Australia)
Northampton
Nottingham (Notts)
Nuneaton
Old Albanians
Old Alleynians
Old Blues
Old Colfeians
Old Cranleighans
Old Elthamians
Old Emmanuel
Old Hamptonians
Old Merchant Taylors
Old Midwhitgiftians
Old Reedonians
Old Wimbledonians
Otago (New Zealand)
Orrell
Otley
Oxford
Oxford University
Paignton
Penryn
Percy Park
Plymouth Albion
Pontypool
Pontypridd
Portsmouth
Preston Grasshoppers
Purley John Fisher
Racing Club de France
R.C.t 'Gool, Numegen (Holland)
Reading
Redruth

R.M.A. Sandhurst
Rosslyn Park
Rotherham
Roundhay
Royal Navy
Rugby
Ruislip
St Girons (France)
St Just
St Luke's College
St Mary's Hospital
Sale
Saracens
Shelford
Sheffield
Sidcup
Southend
Southern Hemisphere (Australia)
South Wales Police
Spanish Combination
Staines
Stevenage
Streatham-Croydon
Swansea
Sudbury
Sutton & Epsom
Tabard

Teignmouth
Thanet Wanderers
Thornbury
Thurrock
Torquay Athletic
Tottonians
Trojans
Tunbridge Wells
University College, Cork
University Vandals
U.S. Portsmouth
Uxbridge
Vale of Lune
Wakefield
Warlingham
Wasps
Waterloo
Westcombe Park
Western Samoa
West Hartlepool
West London Institute
Whitland
Wilmslow
Wimbledon
Winchester
Worthing

Epilogue

The last forty years in the history of the second oldest rugby club in the world have, as you will have read, been marked by many notable facts.

It must be a proud boast of those privileged - whether on or off the field - to sport the coveted old gold, red and black and that it would be hard to find a club that has done more to promote the game of rugby football.

Richmond has nurtured the young from days of mini-rugby to the highest levels of the game and at that pinnacle had provided international players of high repute.

The club, from junior to senior levels has carried the spirit of the game to every continent whilst the Heavies have dispersed their own brand of joi-de-vivre with reckless abandon.

We have excelled - at times - in seven-a-sides and we have taken the distaff side under our wing and helped them to become the talk of boutiques and hairdressers the world over.

And what other club could have risen like Phoenix from the ashes of the damned to the remarkable financial and playing strongholds we are today?

Alan Skeats
2006

"Courageous Richmond, Well Hast Thou Acquit Thee"

(William Shakespeare had foresight!)

The Sun

Many Richmond chapters have ended up in 'The Sun' and, on this page, we add two generations of Sun landlords (and ladies), Vic and Iris Balchin and Joe and Margy Clarke, to the history.

We have tried and failed to calculate the number of man-hours spent by Richmond members in The Sun since 1961 and have similarly failed to calculate consumption volume and total expenditure.

Iris and Vic

Joe with a well-known regular (Margy's in the kitchen)

Wherever you look, including heavenwards, The Sun contains amazing rugby memorabilia. We found this and thought it well worth reproducing as another fine piece of Richmond FC history.

The Original Richmond Normans

BACK ROW JEFF BANNISTER. MIKE HUMPHREYS. STEVE JOLY. MIKE DICK. MATT JEWERS. RICHARD VYVYAN.
MIKE FENNER. BOB SHORTLANDS. MALCOLM ARROWSMITH. DUNCAN WEAVER.
FRONT ROW DAVE HOFMYER. MIKE CHAMBERS. KEVIN WAKEFORD. PETE DUNNING. (CAPT) TIM MARTINEAU.
JOHN DAVIS. TIM GROSSNICKLE. ANNE DUNNING. (TEAM SEC)